CW00392800

Imperfect Knowledge and Monetary Policy

Based on lectures given as part of The Stone Lectures in Economics, this book discusses the problem of formulating monetary policy in practice, under the uncertain circumstances which characterize the real world. The first lecture highlights the limitations of decision rules suggested by the academic literature and recommends an approach involving, first, a firm reliance on the few fundamental and robust results of monetary economics and, secondly, a pragmatic attitude to policy implementation, taking into consideration lessons from central banking experience. The second lecture revisits Milton Friedman's questions about the effects of active stabilization policies on business cycle fluctuations. It explores the implications of a simple model where the policy maker has imperfect knowledge about potential output and the private sector forms expectations according to adaptive learning. This lecture shows that imperfect knowledge limits the scope for active stabilization policy and strengthens the case for conservatism.

OTMAR ISSING is a member of the Executive Board, European Central Bank.

VÍTOR GASPAR is Special Advisor, Banco de Portugal.

ORESTE TRISTANI is Principal Economist, DG Research, European Central Bank.

DAVID VESTIN is Economist, DG Research, European Central Bank.

The Stone Lectures in Economics

Already published:
Statistics, Econometrics and Forecasting – Arnold Zellner

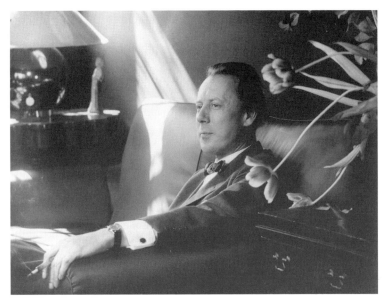

Sir Richard Stone, Nobel Laureate in Economics.

THE STONE LECTURES IN ECONOMICS

Imperfect Knowledge and Monetary Policy

Otmar Issing and Vítor Gaspar
with
Oreste Tristani and David Vestin

CAMBRIDGE UNIVERSITY PRESS

CAMBRIDGE UNIVERSITY PRESS
Cambridge, New York, Melbourne, Madrid, Cape Town, Singapore, São Paulo

Cambridge University Press
The Edinburgh Building, Cambridge CB2 2RU, UK

Published in the United States of America by Cambridge University Press, New York

www.cambridge.org
Information on this title: www.cambridge.org/9780521671071

First published 2005

Printed in the United Kingdom at the University Press, Cambridge

A catalogue record for this book is available from the British Library

ISBN-13 978-0-521-85486-3 hardback
ISBN-10 0-521-85486-5 hardback
ISBN-13 978-0-521-67107-1 paperback
ISBN-10 0-521-67107-8 paperback

Contents

Figures and table

Figures

Table

Acknowledgments

We wish to thank Klaus Adam, Steve Cecchetti, Athanasios Orphanides, Gerhard Rünstler, Frank Smets, and Caroline Willeke for helpful comments and suggestions on a preliminary draft. Sandrine Corvoisier and Björn Fischer provided excellent research assistance. We also wish to thank Patricia Kearns-Endres and Luisa Rey for editorial assistance and the organizers of the Stone Lectures Series at the Bank of England and at the National Institute for Economic and Social Research for their help. A final thank you to Chris Harrison for ensuring a smooth and pleasant interaction between the authors and the publisher.

Introduction

Uncertainty is a pervasive fact of life. Many decisions have to be taken with limited information, imperfect knowledge, in an ever-changing environment.

The decision to purchase any consumption good is always taken based on limited information about, for example, the distribution of prices across retailers. One can cross-check prices from a couple of small shops and large retailers, but very quickly the costs of gathering and processing new information become prohibitively high. Quoting F. H. Knight, "it is evident that the rational thing to do is to be irrational, where deliberation and estimation cost more than they are worth."[1]

Imperfect knowledge also characterizes most important decisions in life. The choice of a university degree course is often made while ignoring one's own chances of actually attaining the degree, the impact of the degree on future job opportunities or the relative merits of the degree when compared with alternatives.

A by-product of imperfect knowledge is that evaluations of future outcomes may be formed in ways that are not necessarily correct. Different people may have different perceptions on the best degree and university. In turn, people's perceptions may affect outcomes, so that "the truth" will not be independent of the learning process by which perceptions are formed. To continue the university analogy, perceptions about the least useful degrees may change over time. A degree perceived as unattractive may actually become unattractive *ex post* – even if it was not *ex ante* – because the demand for graduates will be diverted toward other degree holders and the quality of candidates will deteriorate as fewer and fewer students are interested in a course that "proves" to be unpopular.

The ensuing vicious circle of adverse selection is an example of endogenous dynamics due to the interaction between individual learning, which is necessary to form beliefs about the future, and outcomes. One could speculate that such dynamics would tend to become less relevant over time, as beliefs are validated and decisions improve. The problem, however, is that in a world of learning under imperfect knowledge structural change must be recurrent. As a result, learning dynamics are arguably a perennial feature of the real world. After identifying the cheapest retailer of a specific consumption good, one may realize that a better price is available over the Internet. The learning process must therefore be restarted along this new dimension.

The combination of imperfect knowledge, limited information and learning implies that we are often unable to characterize uncertainty precisely. At the individual level, a large body of experimental evidence has in fact emphasized a number of puzzles emerging when individuals are assumed to behave in ways consistent with the postulates of expected utility theory.[2] The importance and frequency of paradoxes relating to inference and to economic behavior under uncertainty clearly show the limits of intuition on these matters.

As do all other decision makers, central banks have to face these daunting dimensions of uncertainty. More specifically, central banks have limited information on the state of the economy and on the nature, size, and persistence of various disturbances. At the same time, central banks are extremely uncertain about the exact functioning of economies, and notably about the extent and timing of the propagation mechanism of policy actions. While economic research, conducted both in academia and in central banks,[3] has helped to uncover some broad features of the transmission mechanism, recurrent structural breaks imply that what we have learned from the past cannot be trusted to remain useful.

In central banks, moreover, uncertainty reaches a different, more complex dimension. The main reason is that central banks are important players affecting the overall behavior of the economic system. The result is that, for a central bank, the problem of taking decisions under uncertainty is compounded by that of understanding how private agents' behavior will react to such decisions. More concretely, this problem amounts to ensuring that agents' expectations, which will themselves be formed under uncertain conditions and as a result of some learning mechanism, remain appropriately anchored.

Given this powerful interaction of limited information, imperfect knowledge and endogenous expectations under recurrent structural breaks, what is the appropriate course of action for a central bank?

The academic literature has long striven to provide an answer.

A first tentative answer can be obtained by ignoring the complications of imperfect knowledge and structural breaks and focusing on some dimensions of limited information. More specifically, a large literature has provided policy prescriptions based on the assumption that the central bank and private agents have perfect knowledge of the mechanisms that regulate the functioning of the economy. Some of these mechanisms, however, are assumed to be hidden, or observed with noise, and they therefore need to be inferred from other available information.

This sort of uncertainty can arise at different levels. First, it can be due to imperfections in the quality of the data. Some variables may be known only with a time lag; others may be subject to substantial revision over time. Second, uncertainty regards the level of unobservable variables that can be defined within specific models of the economy. Well-known examples are the output gap, the equilibrium real interest rate, the equilibrium exchange rate, and various measures of excess liquidity conditions. Third, and finally, economic models typically include disturbances whose nature, identification, and interpretation are also uncertain. Here uncertainty involves, for example, assessing whether the shocks occur on the demand side or the supply side of the economy and whether they are transitory or persistent.

In these cases, under some additional conditions, the response of theory is that *certainty equivalence* holds.[4] The certainty equivalence principle simply states that optimal policy can be determined as in a world of certainty, provided that unknown variables are replaced by their expected or estimated values. Certainty equivalence also implies that estimation can be separated from the policy decision. The central bank can therefore try to form the best possible assessment of the evolution of the unobservable variables in a first logical stage, and then decide policy, in a second stage, as if the estimated values of the unobservable variables were certain. In this respect, uncertainty causes no problem for decision-making; it just introduces an estimation problem as an extra step.

Certainty equivalence shows that some dimensions of uncertainty can be tackled more easily than one might conjecture *ex ante*. The drawbacks are that these policy prescriptions are applicable only when the correct mechanisms that regulate the functioning of the economy are indeed known, that is when there is no "model uncertainty." The same policy prescriptions may cause large mistakes when model uncertainty is great. An interesting example based on Larson (1999) is illustrative in this respect. He states: "In the age of certainty, at the gateways of the twentieth century, the expected was as good as fact." He then continues: "To turn was every storm's destiny." Larson is telling the story of the hurricane of 8 September 1900 that destroyed most of Galveston.[5]

Conscious of the limitations of the assumption of perfect knowledge of the economy, the academic literature has moved on to consider the implications of deeper forms of uncertainty.

In particular, academia has realized that considerable uncertainty characterizes, first, the quantitative strength of some structural relationships, i.e. the value of parameters which define elasticities and functional dependencies within any particular model. Inevitably, available parameter estimates are affected by data imperfections and by the particular econometric techniques that are employed for estimation. Second, there may be fundamental uncertainty about the overall features of the model that would provide the most appropriate description of the structural relationships in the economy. For example, different variables might be thought to affect the dynamics of inflation, or there may be ambiguity about the exact functional forms of some structural relations.

Traditionally these deeper forms of uncertainty have been modeled using Bayesian decision theory. Authors solve for decision rules that are desirable under some prior on the model parameters. Uncertainty is usually related to policy multipliers or, more generally, to the transmission mechanism of monetary policy. In an optimal policy context, uncertainty about policy multipliers sometimes leads to a "conservative" result, namely a cautious, more muted response of policy instruments to disturbances to the economy, compared with conditions of certainty. The conservatism principle could be intuitively appealing in some contexts, as argued by Alan Blinder (1998), for example. It is, however, by no means applicable to all cases of parameter uncertainty. Uncertainty concerning the dynamic response of the economy, for example, has been shown to warrant a more forceful policy response to shocks than would be implied by certainty equivalence.[6]

Caution can be taken even less for granted when one analyses model uncertainty in general. Model uncertainty poses a truly fundamental challenge. It is a very relevant challenge because there seems to be a substantial lack of agreement on the best model to use for policy purposes. As McCallum (1999) clearly stated, "it is not just that the economics profession does not have a well-tested quantitative model of the quarter-to-quarter dynamics, the situation is much worse than that: we do not even have any basic agreement about the qualitative nature of the mechanism."

A general problem of trying to deal with model uncertainty is that there is not even consensus on how to describe it analytically. Some authors have chosen to analyze the performance of simple monetary policy rules within different macroeconomic models, selected to reflect a wide range of views on aggregate dynamics. This follows a suggestion by McCallum (1997, p. 355): "Because there is a great deal of professional disagreement as to the proper specification of a structural macroeconomic model, it seems likely to be more fruitful to strive to design a policy rule that works reasonably well in a variety of plausible quantitative models, rather than to derive a rule that is optimal in any one particular model." Rules of the former sort can be described as "robust"; they tend to share the feature of incorporating a substantial degree of policy inertia.[7]

An alternative interpretation of robustness has been given in the context of robust control. Various applications have studied the behavior of a policy maker who uses a macroeconomic model, but recognizes that the model is an approximation and is uncertain about the quality of that approximation. In such circumstances, the policy maker will develop a concern for minimizing losses in the worst-case scenarios. Very often, monetary policies developed using the robust control approach have the property of being more aggressive than the optimal policies absent model uncertainty, thus overturning the conservatism principle.[8]

A final, recent strand of literature focuses on the aspects of bounded rationality connected to the interplay of adaptive learning and the endogeneity of expectations. This literature also moves from the observation that rational expectations require an unrealistic degree of knowledge of the structure of the true model and of the parameters. It then goes on to suggest that it is more realistic to assume that agents in the economy, such as empirical economists, have to make inference and run regressions in order to learn parameter values and update their results as new data become available. The outcome is adaptive learning, a process by which agents adapt their forecast rules over time. Adaptive learning introduces to the models additional dynamics that are not present under full rationality. As agents update their forecasts and expectations, their optimal policies and, in turn, equilibrium outcomes will also change. As a result, agents' perceptions of the truth will evolve, generating further changes in behavior and outcomes. If the economy occasionally experiences structural shifts, these additional dynamics will not disappear over time because agents will have to relearn the relevant parameters and processes. In the field of monetary policy, this literature shows that monetary policy must react aggressively to inflationary shocks. The aggressive reaction ensures that agents' expectations, which are endogenous, remain anchored on the central bank's inflation objective.[9]

To summarize, the burgeoning literature on monetary policy under uncertainty has unveiled a number of important results which can represent useful benchmarks in policy discussions.[10] In spite of tremendous progress in a number of directions, however, from an applied perspective most results continue to be model-dependent or based on specific assumptions on the degree of policy makers' and/or individuals' knowledge of the functioning of the economy.

Outline of the two lectures

The pervasive nature of uncertainty in actual monetary policy decision making is the key stylized fact motivating both lectures in this volume. How should central banks set monetary policy? In which way should they take uncertainty into account when designing a monetary policy strategy? Should they be aggressive or cautious in their response to shocks?

Ideally, central banks would like to be able to rely on a set of analytical tools of universal relevance. An example of such analytical tools are national accounts systems, which Richard Stone helped to develop from the early 1940s. Sixty years later it is clear that national accounts systems have greatly contributed to empirical and policy-relevant economic research. Timely and accurate statistics are, in Europe and elsewhere, as important as at the time of Stone's original contributions. Even more remarkably, these contributions, which were part of the dissemination of Keynesian ideas, have been accepted and used by all schools of economic thought. They are, in this respect, robust analytical tools of the type most useful and necessary to all fields of economics, but especially to monetary policy analysis, in view of our great ignorance about the features of real-world economies.

Very few tools in monetary policy analysis possess the same degree of robustness as national accounts systems. A fully scientific approach to monetary policy is therefore impossible, given the current state of knowledge.

The first lecture, a collaboration by Otmar Issing and Oreste Tristani, delivered by Otmar Issing, suggests one possible approach to dealing with the difficulty of bridging the gap between academic knowledge and real-world problems. The approach involves two main components: first, a firm reliance on the few fundamental and robust results of monetary economics; second, a pragmatic attitude to the implementation of policy, which takes due consideration of the lessons learned from central banking experience.

Reliance on the fundamental and robust results of monetary economics entails, first and foremost, ensuring that price expectations remain anchored and that the probability of occurrence of events such as the Great Depression, German hyperinflation and the great inflation of the 1970s remains negligible. In order to achieve this end, it is crucial to base decisions on a clear price stability objective and to attach paramount importance to the goal of maintaining credibility. An important role for money also helps. Reliance on the strong long-run link between money and prices can help to preempt sustained inflation or deflation and to avoid the sort of monetary collapse associated with the Great Depression.

The lessons from central banking experience can help offset our lack of knowledge of the determinants of short-run economic dynamics. This implies that it would be a mistake to focus on any single view of the functioning of monetary economies. When designing its reaction to the day-to-day evolution of economic variables, a central bank will have to rely on its judgment and adopt an eclectic approach. These judgmental elements, and the explicit role for the policy maker's beliefs that they entail, will play an important role in the actual decision-making process. As a result, monetary policy making acquires the "artistic" features that are often emphasized in the literature.

The aforementioned two elements complement each other. The results of central bank independence and the fundamental importance of price stability can be reflected in the institutional framework of the central bank, so guarding society against the risks of a fully discretionary approach to policy. Centuries ago, Kant (1793) remarked that "No man has the right to pretend that he is practically expert in a science and yet show contempt for theory without revealing that he is an ignoramus in his field." At the same time, the judgmental elements are necessary to bridge the gap between the simplifications of monetary theory and the complexities of real-world decision making.

Rather than making the argument along purely conceptual lines, the first lecture couches it in the context of the practical experience of two central banks in two specific historical episodes. The central banks are the Bundesbank and the European Central Bank (ECB) and the episodes are German monetary unification and the start of the single monetary policy in Europe. These episodes have been selected because they are especially interesting in terms of the dimension of uncertainty faced by the central banks. From the viewpoint of monetary policy, both episodes can in fact be classified as examples of "uncharted territory," i.e. of exceptional shocks, from a historical and political viewpoint, that posed a particularly high challenge for the monetary policy makers. They are therefore particularly useful to illustrate how to keep a firm sense of direction while relying on judgment because of limited information and knowledge.

The second lecture, a collaboration by Vítor Gaspar and David Vestin, delivered by Vítor Gaspar, focuses on these aspects and studies some of the factors that can make stabilization policies destabilizing for economic activity and private-sector expectations. More specifically, the lecture uses a small laboratory model to analyze economic dynamics when private-sector expectations are endogenous and the central bank does not directly observe potential output. Initial results from this line of research have been obtained by Orphanides and Williams (2002a, 2003a, 2003b), Gaspar and Smets (2002), and Gaspar, Smets and Vestin (2003).

Based on this literature, the second lecture analyses the consequences of alternative ways of making private-sector expectations endogenous, the role of asymmetric information and the relevance of how the policy makers make inferences about the economy. The results suggest that, when information lags and the possibility of misperceptions of unobservable variables are taken into account, anchoring inflation expectations is of paramount importance for the central bank, in order to avoid sharp deterioration in economic performance.

In order to achieve this objective, the second lecture argues that the central bank should be conservative in the Rogoff (1985) sense. A very low, and much smaller than society's, weight on output-gap stabilization is most often the only way to avoid excess output volatility *ex post*, because it ensures that persistent inflationary or deflationary episodes are avoided and that the economy does not have to bear the large costs of the subsequent return to price stability.

Many of the central themes of the two lectures echo recommendations put forward by Milton Friedman a long time ago and largely confirmed in recent developments of monetary theory. The importance of setting feasible objectives for monetary policy or, as in Friedman (1968), the conscience of "what monetary policy can and cannot do," is a clear example of this correspondence. After a long period of inattention to nominal variables, Friedman reminded economists and central banks that "the monetary authority controls nominal quantities . . . In principle, it can use this control to peg a nominal quantity . . . or to peg the rate of change in a nominal quantity . . . It cannot use its control over nominal quantities to peg a real quantity." This in spite of the fact that "monetary policy can and does have important effects on these real magnitudes" (Friedman, 1968, p. 11).

Another recurrent recommendation in Friedman is on the risks implicit in myopic policies and, in more general terms, in policies based on unrealistic levels of knowledge of business-cycle dynamics and of information on the state and prospects of the economy. One important way in which these policies can be destabilizing is by inducing instability in expectations.

Again consistently with Friedman's lesson, our general message is to be wary of over-ambitious stabilization policies, which often fail to maintain their promises *ex post*. Anchoring nominal variables and establishing and maintaining credibility are the key dimensions on which the success of a central bank must be measured. They represent the best way in which the central bank can also contribute to fostering a stable macroeconomic environment.

1

Monetary policy in uncharted territory

BANK OF ENGLAND, NOVEMBER 3, 2003

"If the world were clear, art would not exist."

(ALBERT CAMUS, THE MYTH OF SISYPHUS)

1.1 Introduction

This lecture focuses on the special difficulties of monetary policy making under realistic levels of uncertainty. The kind of question I have at the back of my mind is not related to the optimal setting of monetary policy *within* a certain model. It is connected to actual decision making and can thus be phrased as follows: how should policy be set given past dynamics and current values of available observable variables? In other words, I realistically acknowledge that, to provide a concrete example, it is not simply the case that the output gap is unobservable and difficult to measure and estimate, but also that both its definition and its role in influencing inflation dynamics are ambiguous.

One problem with trying to answer directly this sort of question is that a formal treatment becomes impossible. I should therefore clarify that I do believe that mathematical models have been beneficial for economics, as they have allowed the discipline to reach results which would have been impossible to achieve without formal methods. Nevertheless, the usefulness of models should never lead us to believe that they are true representations of the world. When formal elegance becomes an end – rather than a means to an end – for theoretical research, theory risks being of little help as a guide for practical decision making. The difficult quest for a model which can be trusted completely as a descriptive – let alone prescriptive – tool for economic policy is still only at its beginning.

The problem of adopting an informal approach is that one risks being imprecise. This is, after all, the reason economists started framing questions within mathematical models, rather than proceeding solely through verbal arguments. The way I deal with this problem in the lecture, and which turns out to be a key feature of the approach I put forward, is to treat formal results as a necessary reference point, while always bearing in mind the limitations of the assumptions based on which they are derived. Consequently, I emphasize and rely heavily upon formal results that are sufficiently general and model independent. On the contrary, I will not discuss, and sometimes I will criticize openly, results that are closely dependent on some details of the specification of a model.

The tension between, on the one hand, the lessons from academic research and, on the other hand, the needs of practical policy making, provides inspiration for the main conclusions of the analysis. I put forward an approach to monetary policy making under uncertainty that involves two main components: first, a firm reliance on the fundamental and robust results of monetary economics; second, a pragmatic attitude to policy implementation, which takes in due consideration lessons from central banking experience.

This topic will be discussed from the viewpoint of an author who has had the privilege of dealing with both the academic and the practical challenges of central banking during his professional life. The discussion is therefore inspired by the practical problems encountered by the economics professor in actual decision making. More specifically, the examples of German unification and European monetary unification (EMU) will be used as concrete reference points in the discussion. There are episodes where the level of uncertainty reached exceptional heights and the limitations of knowledge emerged most strikingly. However extensive one's knowledge of the economy before such events, it is possibly irrelevant afterwards. In the end, one must resign oneself to the need of starting from scratch in the process of trying to understand economic developments.

For a policy maker, as opposed to an academic, the problem is that, while learning and analyzing, decisions still have to be taken. The process reminds me of Neurath's boat, "a boat which we can rebuild only at sea while staying afloat in it" (Quine, 1969, p. 127, quoting Neurath, 1932, p. 206). Decisions have to be made in the face of pervasive uncertainty and in the absence of conclusive evidence. The policy maker has therefore no choice but to bear the "burdens of judgment."

The lecture is organized as follows. Section 1.2 highlights the features of German unification and EMU that make them special in the sense of generating exceptionally high levels of uncertainty. The section also outlines the broad contours of the approach which, I argue, is necessary to cope with such exceptional levels of uncertainty. As already anticipated, the constituent elements of the approach are a firm reliance on research results of general relevance and a concrete attitude in the short-run implementation of policy.

I elaborate on such two elements in sections 1.3 and 1.4, respectively. More specifically, section 1.3 spells out the components of the suggested approach to monetary policy making that can be seen as more direct applications of principles and results of general relevance. These components are related to the need to ensure a nominal anchor for the economy and for agents' expectations, and to guard from the risks of short-term oriented discretionary policy. Section 1.4 focuses instead on those elements of the approach where the guidance of theory is less clear and the policy maker must rely more on practical experience in order to make progress.

Sections 1.5 and 1.6 provide concrete examples of the suggested approach, namely the monetary policies of the Bundesbank and the ECB. In both cases, I provide a short description of the monetary policy strategies adopted by the two central banks, viewed as two different applications of my suggested approach. I then describe some special challenges faced by the two institutions, with a view to highlighting how a more orthodox approach could be costly. Each section ends with a short assessment of the two experiences.

Section 1.7 concludes with a brief summary of the main lessons which can be drawn from the Bundesbank and ECB experiences.

1.2   Uncharted territory: unique historical events

This section begins with a review of the elements that make unique historical events, such as German unification and EMU, "special" in terms of the level and nature of uncertainty they induce, as compared with the "ordinary" levels and forms of uncertainty discussed in the introduction. Understanding such peculiarities is arguably essential in order to devise an appropriate monetary policy strategy to deal with them.

I then move on to discuss why pretence of a fully scientific attitude to monetary policy is inferior, in practice, to an approach complemented by judgmental elements, especially when unique historical events take place.

1.2.1   The special nature of unique historical events

Economic systems are constantly in motion, either because of the occurrence of shocks or as a result of the adjustment process triggered by shocks that occurred in the past. It is important, therefore, to clarify in what sense the fundamental economic change occurring at the time of unique historical events retains a special nature with respect to other shocks that normally affect the economy. In general, a shock will be considered "historical"when it incorporates two main features.

First and foremost, it needs to coincide with an actual or perceived regime shift in policy, i.e. a regime shift in the classical sense of Lucas (1976). A typical example of a regime shift occurs when central banks adopt or change their monetary policy strategy. However, I will also speak of perceived regime shift when agents come to *expect* a change in the monetary policy strategy under the influence of a unique historical event, and without an explicit announcement in this sense by the central bank or the government.

As shown by Lucas (1976), the fundamental problem of policy regime shifts is that agents' behavior and expectations are not independent of the shift. In the practice of monetary policy making, this problem often becomes apparent in the need to (re)gain credibility after the regime shift. The risk is that inflation expectations can move out of line with the inflation objective of the central bank. High inflation expectations, in turn, will lead to actual high inflation, thus becoming entrenched and starting an inflationary spiral.

German unification and EMU can certainly be classified as regime shifts. In the first case, this is because it was unclear, at least *ex ante*, whether the policy strategy of the Bundesbank would have to change to cope with the specific challenge posed by the political choice to merge two economies so different that they could be in different worlds. In the case of EMU the regime shift was more direct, since unification implied the abolition of national currencies, the introduction of a single one and the establishment of a new monetary policy authority. Indeed, the launch of the euro meant that eleven national money markets, characterized by a variety of participants, operating conventions, settlement structures, and credit facilities, merged into a single one almost overnight.[1] The ECB, a new central bank, had to establish its own credibility amidst scepticism on whether the euro would be a stable currency and some predictions that the new monetary union would break down before ordinary citizens could even see its notes and coins.

The second important feature considered necessary to define a shock as radical economic change is that the shock must be a rare, "historical" event, affecting the political sphere as well as the economic environment. The implication is that potentially permanent modifications of structural relationships characterizing the evolution of the economy may take place even irrespective of a policy regime shift. Uncertainty on how expectations will react to changes caused by a "unique" event can reach new heights.

This second feature sets apart the experiences of German unification and, especially, EMU from those of other central banks dealing with potential or actual policy regime shifts. In spite of the severity of the crises faced by some countries at the time of a policy regime shift, the nature of such crises was better known. Large exchange-rate devaluations, for example, were recurring events which had already occurred in the recent past in many European countries. Similar considerations apply to sharp increases in policy interest rates. Such circumstances were certainly not easy to deal with for policy makers, but they were not unprecedented.

German unification and EMU were, to the contrary, unique historical events.

For Germany, unification implied the merging of two quite different economies, an increase in population of approximately 25 percent (from 62 million to 79 million) and an increase in GDP which was initially estimated at approximately 10 percent but later turned out to be substantially lower. The introduction of the DM in the former East Germany on 1 July 1990 required a huge one-time expansion of the German money supply. The second event, EMU, created from scratch a new currency for a large economy of dimensions similar in size to the United States and with a larger population. This new monetary area emerged from the collation of a number of economies, most of which could be described as small and very open.

In both cases, monetary unification took place concurrently with other factors leading to the transformation of the economy in general, and the financial system in particular. Thus, all known structural relationships could change permanently, from price and wage setting, to the sensitivity of aggregate demand to interest-rate changes and the whole monetary policy transmission mechanism.

At the time of unification, the debate in Germany focused in particular on the possibility of instability in the demand for money.[2] The debate, however, subsumed the uncertainties over the outcome of the profound transformation undergone by East Germany. Monetary unification meant transition to a market economy and introduction of a modern financial and banking system in the formerly socialist East German economy. Private entrepreneurs were suddenly facing funding needs, households were offered a whole array of financial assets. This situation left the Bundesbank facing manifold sources of uncertainty. On the one hand, the West German system was simply extended to encompass the eastern *Länder*. On the other hand, it was unclear how East Germans would have behaved under the new market economy in a variety of respects, including portfolio choices which were of key relevance in assessing the stability of the demand for money. Both demand patterns in general and relative prices could be expected to vary significantly after the removal of distortions imposed on the economy by the communist regime. This source of uncertainty was aggravated by the lack of an appropriate national accounting system, which meant that real output and prices could be measured only with a large margin of error. These uncertainties were compounded by the risks to credibility posed by the public clash between the Bundesbank and the government over the terms of unification.

The structural change implicit in the creation of the euro area was, first, of a larger scale, as it involved many countries. In addition, the euro area has evidently different features from those of its constituent countries. For one, the euro area is "large" in terms of its weight in world GDP and relatively closed to international trade. In 2002, the GDP of EU member states totalled approximately 7 billion euros, a figure comparable to, even if lower than, the 9 billion euros (at PPP exchange rates) of the United States. In 2002 the degree of openness, as measured by the average of exports and imports of goods and services as a percentage of GDP, was approximately 19 percent in the euro area. While larger than in the United States and Japan, where the corresponding figure is 11 percent in both cases, this degree of openness is significantly lower than in any member state whose major trade takes place with other euro area countries.

Additionally, all countries participating in EMU were in an ongoing process of evolution due to the economic integration triggered by the creation of the single market. The "convergence criteria" for participation in EMU had already led to low inflation and interest rates, stable intra-EU exchange rates, and the necessary degree of fiscal consolidation in the prospective euro area countries. In spite of the occurrence of shocks such as the ERM crisis of 1992–3, at the end of 1998 all national central banks of prospective euro area countries had in fact succeeded in bringing inflation under control. It was not clear, however, whether national policies would all continue to be set in ways consistent with fiscal prudence. On a more general note, the real convergence process associated with the establishment of the single currency could be expected to continue with renewed strength after the abolition of national currencies. This implied the possibility of a persistent change in the structure of the economy over many years.

As a result, it was unclear how the euro area economy would behave under the new monetary union, and it was impossible to rely on the help of econometrics to shed light on this issue because of data uncertainties – as well as because of the structural break. In fact, the creation of the euro area introduced a strong discontinuity in the available statistical information. Consequently, any econometric analysis of the euro area as a whole must still be based on partly synthetic aggregates, created ad hoc in a manner that raises methodological and conceptual problems. Furthermore, the set of statistics available for the euro area was initially much more restricted than what is normally available to the central bank of any industrial country.

A related difficulty faced by the ECB was the institutional and cultural change implicit in the new institution, which added to the complexity of its analytical and communication framework. The ECB was a new central bank with a new decision-making body. Many observers feared *ex ante* that the Governing Council might be too slow in taking decisions because of its size and composition, or that a number of voting coalitions would immediately be created, so that decisions would ultimately be in the national interests of the winning coalition rather than in the interest of the area as a whole. The internal process of analysis and filtering of economic information that leads to the assessment of the future risks to price stability by the decision-making bodies had to be shaped from scratch. Finally, in terms of communication special difficulties stemmed from the need to deal with many languages and cultures. Over time, different participating central banks had developed different ways to communicate with "their" public, implying that the ECB message could acquire different connotations and ultimately be perceived differently in different countries.[3]

1.2.2   *Dealing with unique historical events*

Historical events of the sort described so far are sufficiently rare to place central bankers in uncharted territory. They impart a profound discontinuity in the data and make econometric inference especially hard. They increase the level of uncertainty to extraordinary peaks. They raise doubts about most features of the existing decision-making process in place before their occurrence. All this in the midst of possible instability in private sector behavior.

The main implication of having to deal with such situations of extreme uncertainty is that of broadening the gap between the assumptions of academic theories and models and the more complex features of reality. The models provide us with a range of illustrative results, which hold only under very specific sources of uncertainty. If, realistically, one mixed many sources of uncertainty, one would find it difficult to come to any robust prescription from theory. An illustrative example is the celebrated Brainard (1967) paper on conservatism in the face of parameter uncertainty. Brainard clarifies there that "For our purpose, a structural change is described by the way it changes the joint distribution of the parameters . . . The task of determining how the imposition of some new regulation or the emergence of some new financial market alters that distribution is obviously a major one and beyond the scope of this paper" (p. 422).

Given the current state of academic knowledge, a policy maker asked to take decisions using only model-based results would have to face the fact that different models often provide different quantitative, and possibly even qualitative, policy implications. In order to make progress, policy makers have to complement the available knowledge of model-based results with their best judgment. Decisions will partly be guided by general and robust theoretical results, and partly be informed by the policy makers' beliefs on the determinants and effects of a particular development.

A limited reliance on judgmental elements is what allows the decision maker to act, based on information that is always too limited and knowledge that is always inadequate. If such elements were banned from policy making, any conscientious decision maker would always conclude that further results are needed before dealing with any practical problem. The judgmental elements are akin to Emmanuel Kant's "contingent belief," i.e. a belief based on one's best assessment of a complex situation.

One way in which beliefs can help is, for example, by producing better-informed decisions. Beliefs can in fact incorporate soft information, which is difficult to capture in records, alongside hard information such as macroeconomic data collected by statistical agencies, which is the sort of information, that typically enters economic models. For a central banker, examples of soft information could be represented by informal evidence of a forthcoming weakening of the economic cycle gathered through talks with various economic and social parties. What central banker would confidently disregard altogether repeated claims from various economic sources that the economy is entering a recession *just* because no hard statistical evidence confirms them?

There are obviously risks in relying on soft information for decision making (see Mullainathan, 2002, for an attempt to model individual behavior based on hard and soft information). A clear risk, well known in experimental psychology, is the possibility of overreaction. An example would be a hasty loosening of monetary conditions in the rest of the world because of deflation in Japan. Similarly, a sequence of interest rate cuts in the USA would raise fears of a "too little, too late" policy response in Europe and trigger a similar sequence of cuts. As shown by recent monetary policy experience, however, these risks tend to materialize more in newspaper articles than in monetary policy decisions.

The remaining sections of this lecture will describe in more detail the main features of my suggested approach to monetary policy. To summarize, the approach is based on the combination of two main ingredients.

The first is a firm reliance on the fundamental and robust results of monetary economics. This implies a strong emphasis on the importance of independence, credibility, and price stability, the ultimate link between inflation and money growth, and the existence of long and variable transmission lags. The consequence is an effort to anchor expectations in a changing environment and to dispel uncertainty about current and future actions of the central bank. In turn, these goals lead to the attribution of overriding importance to a clearly defined price stability objective and a strong focus on medium- and long-term outcomes, rather than the optimization of short-term trade-offs.

The second element of the approach is a pragmatic attitude to policy implementation, i.e. the reliance on the act of judgment to build the bridge from general theoretical results to policy actions. Where the first ingredient of the approach emphasizes and relies on theoretical results, the second is based on the acknowledgment of the limitations of economic theory, in particular concerning our understanding of short-term dynamics of prices and economic activity and of the transmission mechanism. The consequences are a certain amount of scepticism in the application of theoretical results on how to optimally balance short-term trade-offs and the belief that, once the fundamental benefits of medium- and long-run price stability have been attained, the additional gains produced by such "optimized" policies are small, and often model-dependent.

Consistently with the aforementioned features of my suggested approach, in the next two sections I will emphasize a key distinction between the level objective of a central bank and its contribution to ensuring that economic volatility is kept low. The level objective only concerns inflation and it is today reflected in the statutes of many central banks, including the Bundesbank and the ECB. In their pursuit of price stability, however, central banks would also try to avoid inducing excess volatility in inflation, output and interest rates. The latter are sometimes referred to as "volatility objectives."

Accordingly, the discussion in section 1.3 of the robust elements of the approach will be framed mainly in terms of the level objective. The discussion in section 1.4 will instead focus on how to avoid inducing excess volatility in inflation, output, and interest rates.

1.3   Achieving price stability

The mandate of most modern central banks attaches primary relevance to the objective of price stability.[4] The primary concern of central banks is therefore to design monetary policy strategies that allow them to achieve the price stability objective. Two obstacles have to be overcome along the way. The first one, often discussed but arguably of lesser relevance, is represented by exogenous shocks which could cause short-term deviations from price stability. The recent academic literature is fraught with recommendations on how to minimize such deviations. By and large, however, the literature takes the point around which deviations are to be minimized as exogenously given and agreed upon by private agents. The second, and potentially much more dangerous, obstacle which could prevent the central bank from achieving the price stability objective is related to the possibility that private expectations cease to be coordinated on price stability and become focused on an inflationary or deflationary path.

The problem of anchoring expectations is the focus of this section. Its fundamental importance stems from the key role played by expectations in shaping economic dynamics. The central bank often wonders about the reaction of economic agents and financial markets to its own policy decisions and announcements. Conversely, economic agents may be unsure about the precise motivations and actions of central banks and other economic agents. This is always the case, even if market developments are fairly close to what would be expected on the basis of fundamentals.

In the realm of monetary policy, the level of uncertainty stemming from the dynamics of expectations is mainly, and inversely, related to central bank credibility. The more credible a central bank, the more predictable its actions and, in turn, the reactions of the private sector. Conversely, a central bank with little credibility will find it more difficult to plan its own actions because of the uncertain response of economic agents, and it will end up producing further noise in the economic system. It is in this respect that credibility assumes a vital role.

The academic literature has clearly emphasized the key role of credibility and anchoring agents' expectations. In this section I review the main contributions to this literature and then clarify the role they play in shaping key features of good monetary policy strategies.

1.3.1   The importance of anchoring expectations

Anchoring expectations and the inflationary bias
The traditional results on the importance of ensuring that expectations remain focused on the central bank's price stability objective have been obtained within the literature on the time inconsistency of optimal monetary policy. This literature, originating from Kydland

and Prescott (1977), has pointed out that discretionary optimization risks creating an inflation bias. If the central bank has an incentive to create surprise inflation – typically because of its vain attempt to push output above its equilibrium level – the public will take such an incentive into account when forming expectations. The result is that expectations will be inconsistent with the central bank's objective and equilibrium inflation will be higher than the objective.

A vast literature has since concentrated on devising incentive-compatible institutional arrangements capable of enforcing a rule-like behavior on the monetary policy authority. A general feature of the proposed arrangements is to establish an independent central bank in charge of monetary policy, a feature reflected in the statutes of many modern central banks. Another general feature of these arrangements is that the central banks should commit forever to a simple instrument rule "at the beginning of time," and then simply implement monetary policy consistently with that simple rule. This arrangement, however, would be very costly for a number of reasons and it is therefore not seriously considered by any modern society. An arguably more realistic characterization of commitment has recently been offered by Woodford (2003):

> rule-based policymaking as the term is intended here means that at each decision point an action is taken which conforms to a policy rule, which rule is itself one that is judged to be optimal (from a "timeless perspective" . . .) given the central bank's understanding of the monetary transmission mechanism . . . The desire to follow a rule (and so to avoid the trap of discretionary optimization) . . . simply means that whenever this question is taken up, the bank should consider what an optimal rule of conduct would be, rather than asking what an optimal action is on the individual occasion.

A normative result emerging from this literature (see Persson and Tabellini, 1999) is that the goal of pursuing price stability deserves a special emphasis in the statute or mandate of a central bank.

"Intuitively, the whole purpose of optimal contracts is to remove an inflation bias. This is most easily done by means of a direct penalty on inflation, rather than in a more roundabout way, by targeting other variables that are only loosely related to inflation" (Persson and Tabellini, 1999, p. 1435). An inflation objective is also easy to monitor, which enhances accountability.

Finally, it has been pointed out that the central bank should take the natural output level as given when setting policy. If credible, such commitment would in itself solve the inflationary bias problem.

More recent contributions have shown that, if forward-looking variables exist in the economy, credibility has additional benefits to that of eliminating the inflationary bias. Such benefits, however, are in terms of improving inflation and output trade-offs. They are therefore discussed in section 1.4.

Anchoring expectations and endogenous expectations dynamics

In the rational expectations literature, provided that the inflation bias problem is solved, private sector expectations are usually assumed to remain consistent with the central bank's objective. In other words, provided that the central bank has no incentive to create surprise inflation, there is no reason for the public to have doubts about the ultimate return of inflation to the level consistent with the central bank objective. There is therefore no reason for long-term inflation expectations to deviate from the objective.

Such a description of the world is, however, not necessarily realistic. For example, it is not inconceivable that inflation expectations would become unanchored in the face of a prolonged sequence of inflationary shocks. If inflation remained for many years above some level perceived as consistent with the central bank objective, expectations could start factoring in the possibility that the central bank objective is actually higher than previously thought (see Ellingsen and Söderström, 2001, for a simple model where a mechanism of this sort plays a role). Alternatively, agents may start revising their beliefs on the policy horizon of the central bank, in such a way that the return to price stability in the distant future will have a negligible effect on expectations compared with the current inflation level.

What are the consequences to policy of assuming arguably more realistic expectations formation mechanisms? A recent strand of literature has pointed out that economic agents are themselves uncertain about the structure of the economy and the behavior of the central bank. Their inflation expectations will be affected by their view on these issues, possibly evolving over time in response to economic developments.

These ideas have been formalized in the context of the literature on learning when the macroeconomic environment may be changing over time (Evans and Honkapohja, 2001). In a recent paper, Orphanides and Williams (2002a) study a model economy in which agents have to estimate the model parameters to form their inflation expectations. In so doing, agents are assumed to have finite memory – that is, to disregard old data as uninteresting for the current economic regime. At the same time, Orphanides and Williams entertain the possibility that the central bank could be more or less concerned about deviations of inflation from target, relative to deviations of output from potential.

Their results show that the model can lead to a dramatic decoupling of inflation expectations from the policy-maker targets if the policy response to inflation is not sufficiently aggressive. Once inflation expectations become unanchored, a much tighter policy stance is necessary to return to price stability, so that high inflation is accompanied by a recession. The initially less aggressive response to inflation, aimed at smoothing cyclical fluctuations, is the cause of an especially prolonged negative cycle. Such inflation and output dynamics can help to explain the stagflation of the 1970s, a phenomenon which would allegedly not have arisen in many countries if central banks had responded more aggressively to deviations from price stability.

A firm response to inflationary shocks is therefore a necessary condition to ensure that inflation expectations remain anchored in the face of ongoing shocks.

These results appear to be robust to a number of extensions. Orphanides and Williams (2003b) show that, under learning, exogenous shocks can give rise to significant and persistent deviations of inflation expectations from those implied by rational expectations. Orphanides and Williams (2003a) analyze the interaction between private endogenous learning and central bank misperceptions on the natural unemployment rate. Using a similar expectations formation mechanism, Gaspar and Smets (2002) obtain comparable results within a forward-looking model. Gaspar, Smets and Vestin (2003) extend the model further and allow agents to use a richer information set when forming expectations. This set-up is also adopted in the second lecture, where uncertainty on the output gap level is taken into account in the analysis.

1.3.2   Anchoring expectations and key characteristics of a strategy

In order to reap the benefits of credibility and anchor inflation expectations, good monetary policy making should incorporate three main features: primacy to the price stability objective, rule-based behavior implying a systematic response to economic developments, and a firm response to inflationary shocks.

Most of these results have been developed contemporaneously to the implementation in many central banks of reforms aimed at limiting discretion and emphasizing the control of inflation as an overriding objective. This is why "inflation-focused" monetary policy strategies (in the words of Bernanke and Mishkin, 1997) have been characterized as "constrained discretion," as compared with the theoretical notions of pure discretion and full commitment.

The rest of this sub-section discusses the main elements of the inflation-focused approach. Most of these elements are similar across central banks and monetary policy strategies. Other elements represent distinguishing features between strategies.

A public announcement

The first important implication of the theoretical literature on the benefits of credibility is that it is beneficial to adopt the monetary policy strategy through a public announcement. In this respect, the specific characteristics of the strategy of choice are less important – within limits that I shall clarify shortly.

Credibility is not the sole guiding principle behind the decision of many central banks to adopt an explicit monetary policy strategy. A related order of concerns has to do with the willingness to reduce the overall level of uncertainty in the economy by dispelling uncertainty on the actions of the central bank. In fact, economic agents also have to deal with an environment of uncertainty when taking decisions, especially when decisions have an intertemporal dimension or imply commitments on future actions.

The formal adoption of a strategy would prove to be entirely unnecessary if all the details of the functioning of the economy – from policy multipliers to exact transmission lags – were perfectly and commonly known and if all shocks were observed by all agents. In this simple world depicted by many theoretical models, the central bank could simply go on and literally maximize an appropriately selected objective function. The public would then quickly realize what the central bank is doing and form expectations consistently.

In reality, however, the central bank has only, at best, a broad-brush idea of the various channels of the transmission mechanism, and it knows, at the same time, that the prevalent channel may change depending on circumstances. The result is that Milton Friedman's assertion about the long and variable lags of the transmission mechanism remains valid. At the same time, economic agents have to take decisions in an equally uncertain environment.

In this intricate territory, a strategy helps the central bank to dispel the uncertainty linked to its own actions. The effort to characterize the systematic features of the approach followed by the central bank also has the objective of reducing the overall level of uncertainty.

At the end of 1974, the Bundesbank was first, along with the Swiss National Bank, to adopt a formal monetary policy strategy – in both cases, monetary targeting. The most important achievement was to realize that the public announcement of the monetary policy strategy, and the stability of the strategy over time, were elements of crucial importance to avoid introducing noise into the economic system, and to help to maintain credibility and anchor the expectations of economic agents.

As argued in Issing (1997), maintaining a consistent and successful strategy over time may have helped to foster the stability of the monetary system as a whole. The less-pronounced inflation outbursts experienced in Germany, relative to other industrial countries, may have reduced the incentive to substitute money in private portfolios with other assets better protected against the effects of inflation. This, in turn, would have enhanced the stability of estimated money demand relationships, and validated the necessary conditions for the choice of the monetary targeting strategy *ex post*.

The Bundesbank's pioneering experience was followed by many other central banks in the 1990s. While the particular features of the strategy of choice have often been different – from the highly fashionable inflation targeting to the stability-oriented strategy of the ECB – most central banks have chosen to adopt their monetary policy strategy formally, through a public announcement. The long-run performance of the other strategies remains untested, but the Bundesbank experience continues to serve as guidance for all other central banks.

Clearly understood inflation objective

A second key ingredient shared by many strategies over time is the announcement of a clear inflation objective.

The importance of maintaining price stability has long been clear to economists, in relation to the fundamental role played by money as "unit of account" for the value of transactions. In the classical presentations of the theory of money it was stressed that the usefulness of a unit of account depends on the stability of its value. For a given (and approximately constant) stock of a certain commodity (e.g. gold), the stability of prices – or, equivalently, of the value of money – in terms of the commodity was a matter that could be dealt with through institutional means. It was analogous to the use of standard measurement units for distance or weight (e.g. Wicksell, 1935).

The focus on price stability of many central banks has also been validated by the new theoretical developments on dynamic general equilibrium models with nominal frictions, which show that price stability represents the key way in which central banks can help improve the functioning of the economic system (Woodford, 2003).

The advantage of selecting a precise figure for the rate of inflation to be considered consistent with price stability also constitutes an important step toward achieving accountability. By increasing the transparency of the central bank's objective, a numerical definition of price stability also increases the incentive for the central bank to attain it. Finally, a quantified primary objective helps to coordinate inflationary expectations, thus facilitating the achievement of the price stability goal in a world in which agents are forward looking.

Many central banks have made the objective of price stability precise through the announcement of a quantitative definition. In the case of the Bundesbank, this was implicit in the derivation of the monetary target, which was based on a technical assumption on the "normative rate of inflation" (for further details see section 1.5). For the ECB, the primary objective of price stability was clarified at the outset upon announcement of the monetary policy strategy, through the specification of a numerical definition of what exactly should be interpreted as price stability in the euro area and the timeframe over which the central bank is to deliver it (see section 1.6). Similar clarifications have been made by inflation targeting central banks.

There is some evidence showing that a quantitative definition may not be strictly necessary to convey the focus on price stability of the central bank (Castelnuovo, Nicoletti-Altimari and Rodríguez-Palenzuela,

2003). The famous definition proposed by Alan Greenspan (1989), "price levels sufficiently stable so that expectations of change do not become major factors in key economic decisions," can be seen exactly as an attempt to convey the anti-inflationary resolve of the Fed without, at the same time, providing a precise quantitative indication. Presumably, this choice reflects the view that the quantification of the objective of price stability also involves potential costs. The potential costs come from the fact that the economic profession has not come to an agreement on the inflation rate that would ideally maximize economic welfare. Both theoretical and practical arguments can be made in support of and against an inflation rate exactly equal to zero (possibly through a price level objective), or a small positive rate of inflation.

Consistently with more recent theoretical developments (Goodfriend and King, 2000; Woodford, 2003), I would, however, maintain that a numerical definition remains a first best to ensure that the price stability objective is clearly understood and embodied in expectations. There are in fact advocates of a quantitative definition of price stability for the USA, also (e.g. Goodfriend, 2003).

Ensuring that the level inflation objective is achieved

A public adoption of the monetary policy strategy and a numerical definition of price stability are important elements of commitment for any central bank. They are not sufficient mechanisms, however, to ensure that the level inflation objective is achieved, i.e. that inflation expectations remain focused on the objective.

In this respect, the adoption of an aggressive policy response to inflationary or deflationary shocks is useful. An aggressive response helps to maintain private sector expectations anchored to price stability and, at the same time, to avoid second-round price effects and even to mitigate the impact of the original shocks. Such a "hawkish" response, which *ex ante* implies little concern over the output consequences of any policy tightening, often turns out to also minimize the volatility of output over long periods of time. By avoiding prolonged inflationary or deflationary spirals, it also ensures that the economy never needs to bear the cost of the painful measures necessary to return to price stability.

While the aggressive response to deviations from price stability should help, a more general difficulty in anchoring expectations is that the academic literature tends to remain silent on how large deviations from price stability get started and become entrenched. Zero inflation is the point around which model dynamics are often studied and the question asked in the literature is how to make the return to zero inflation after small shocks more or less fast, or more or less costly in terms of some welfare criterion. Such issues are certainly important in terms of the relative volatility in inflation, output, and interest rates which will be discussed in section 1.4. They become, however, of second order when compared with the fundamental problem of how to avoid *true* inflation or deflation – that is, inflationary or deflationary spirals.

It may be argued that prolonged inflation and deflation are relatively rare events, so central bankers can normally act based mainly on a concern for inflation volatility. This is, however, only known *ex post* in practical monetary policy making. *Ex ante*, any small and temporary inflationary shock can potentially reveal itself as the source of an inflationary spiral. And while rarer than small temporary shocks, prolonged inflation and deflation did occur all too frequently in the last century.

Understanding the deep mechanisms that ignite and propagate inflation and deflation is of fundamental importance for a central bank. Which kind of processes or shocks can, if not controlled in time, induce a misalignment between inflationary expectations and the inflation objective? What other processes or shocks can, instead, be dealt with without having to worry about the possibility that they become entrenched in inflationary expectations? Such questions are especially relevant at times of structural and institutional breaks, since these are times when an imperfect alignment of expectations with the inflation objective is most likely. From the viewpoint of central banks, these are also times when lack of precise knowledge about the functioning of the economy could lead to mistaking the beginning of an inflationary or deflationary spiral for yet another temporary price blip.

Given the state of knowledge at the beginning of the 1970s, the Bundesbank resorted to two simple principles to give a sense of direction to its policy. First and foremost, the fundamental theoretical result of monetary neutrality, corroborated by extensive evidence of the one-to-one long-run relationship between inflation and money growth. Second, the dictum that inflation is always and everywhere a monetary phenomenon, i.e. a conscious assumption of responsibility on the central banks' ability to determine inflation in the medium and long run.

By and large, these "old theories" continue to provide a guideline by which to assess whether any price development risks representing the beginning of an inflationary or deflationary spiral. The underlying identity which always holds and which accounts for the inflation level over time remains based on the fundamental link between money prices and the money supply. This link is usually illustrated via the quantity equation, which can be written as

$$\pi_t = \Delta m_t + \Delta v_t - \Delta y_t$$

where π_t represents the inflation rate, and Δm_t, Δv_t, and Δy_t represent the rates of growth of nominal money, velocity, and real output, respectively.

The fundamental message of the quantity equation is that, since real output growth is constrained by technology and if velocity shocks are not large and permanent, sustained inflation can take place only when money growth is high.

An important role of the quantity equation is, incidentally, consistent with the findings of Sir Richard Stone. In his Nobel lecture, Sir Richard emphasized that accounting can be useful "in describing *and understanding* society" (emphasis added): "by organising our data in the form of accounts we can obtain a coherent picture of the stocks and flows, incomings and outgoings of whatever variables we are interested in [. . .] and thence proceed to analyse the system of which they form part" (Stone, 1984).

Many practical experiences confirm that the fundamental arithmetics of the quantity equation do incorporate useful, albeit not always easy to extract, information. Issing (2002) illustrates this point with a simple descriptive exercise based on three selected historical episodes: the Federal Reserve's management of the "roaring 20s" and of the ensuing depression; Japan's monetary policy during the asset price boom of the second half of the 1980s; and monetary policy in Europe during the same period. With the benefit of hindsight, all these episodes suggest that monetary developments would have provided useful information on the impending risks to price stability, over and above the information provided by a simple rule of the Taylor type. The information coming from money was, however, neglected in all cases, with consequences that are *ex post* well known.[5]

In spite of this evidence, many economists remain skeptical about the usefulness of money, ultimately because it is difficult to understand its information content in real time. A central bank can never be sure that a certain monetary development at any point in time is signaling, for example, risks of deflation, rather than being attributable to yet another velocity shock. There are many historical episodes during which monetary growth temporarily out of line with fundamentals did not ignite or boost an inflationary or deflationary process.

These are fair criticisms, as any central bank trying to extract information from money is acutely aware. But they do not imply that we should abandon the role of money simply because we find it difficult to understand in a timely fashion the information it conveys. The usefulness of money comes, to some extent, from the simple fact that its analysis imposes yet another constraint on one's interpretation of the data, if that interpretation is to be framed within a coherent scheme.

Monetary analysis, namely a continuous monitoring of the liquidity conditions in the economy based on information from, e.g., a broad monetary aggregate and its determinants as well as from the components and counterparts of other monetary aggregates, can thus play a useful role in the approach of any central bank willing to pay attention to it. It is in fact an important component of the stability-oriented strategy adopted by the European Central Bank.

A transparent communication framework

An additional way in which central banks can increase the commitment-type features of their monetary policy strategy is by selection of an appropriate, transparent communication policy. Communication represents the specific language that the central bank uses to explain to the public its assessment, based on the strategy, of the current state of and prospects for the economy and the reasoning behind policy decisions. For this reason, the communication policy represents an important complement to the strategy, since it helps to define it more precisely over time for the benefit of the public.

Consistently with the different strategies adopted over time and across countries, different central banks have sometimes chosen to emphasize different particular pieces of information, or elements of their decision making, in their communication policies. Monetary targeting and inflation targeting, in particular, represent the most often discussed benchmarks of recent periods. To these strategies correspond two alternative communication languages used to improve the mutual understanding between the central bank and the public. The publication of the monetary growth figures and of the inflation forecast, respectively, provide a convenient focal point around which the central bank's explanations are organized. Official publications, i.e. long and detailed explanations of the information processing that underlies policy decisions, are in both cases a key component of the communication process.

This is one of those instances where there is no clear guidance from theory.[6] Recent academic contributions have favored the option of organizing the explanations around inflation forecasts. The forecast would ensure maximum transparency because, within a model, it would incorporate all information relevant for the assessment of the risks to price stability. In practice, however, a model-based inflation forecast, however elaborate, tells only parts of the whole story. The ultimately judgmental nature of the sensible forecasts made by all central banks implies that it is never obvious how macroeconomic news feeds into the central bank forecast at each point in time. Hence, the mapping from exogenous information and news to the inflation forecast can never be truly transparent. In particular, no mechanistic reaction to deviations of the forecast from target at a given horizon can be expected from policy. It is ultimately a matter of faith to believe that the forecast numbers indeed convey a complete and truthful representation of the policy maker's evaluation process. As emphasized by Vickers (1999), an outside observer could naturally perceive the risks of "painting by numbers" or "numbers by painting."

Judgmental inputs are also part of communication policies based on the rate of growth of money. The main difference with respect to communication policies based on the inflation forecast is on the logical stage when they are used. For inflation forecasts, the judgment is an integral part of the construction of the forecast. For money growth, statistical outcomes are published first, and the judgmental exercise on their implications for price stability is carried out in a separate, successive step. The assessment on which process is more transparent is, by and large, affected by historical conventions and preferences, rather than by objective arguments.

One advantage of monetary targeting is to bring to the fore the distinction between the inflation level objective and the concern to limit inflation volatility. Medium-term inflation developments are presented as ultimately due to monetary developments determined by the central bank. Inflation targeting, on the other hand, tends to blur the distinction between inflation level and volatility. Medium-term developments are presented as the result of a pure succession of random shocks buffered by the central bank. In monetary targeting, the emphasis is on the ultimately monetary nature of inflation accommodation; in inflation targeting, the accent is on the existence of multiple, often "real," sources of inflation. The ECB strategy borrows elements from both these approaches. From monetary targeting, it takes the emphasis on the level objective, which is reflected in the accentuation of the long-run link between inflation and money growth. From inflation targeting, it draws the emphasis on the need to analyze all relevant information and attempt to combine it in a synthetic, though not all-encompassing, indicator such as the inflation forecast. Using a multiplicity of explanatory tools should ultimately help to provide a more transparent and complete, though not oversimplified, picture of reality. A commitment to continuously justify monetary policy decisions in terms of the evolution of many variables, rather than only with reference to a single indicator, also represents another element which constrains the discretion of the central bank.

In the end, the only general principle in the field of communication is that achieving the maximum degree of transparency is not simply a question of making the maximum amount of information available. "What matters most in order to make sense of reality (which is inherently non-transparent to policy makers and the public alike) and of policy makers' behaviour is a coherent frame of reasoning to interpret the subset of *relevant* information through *clear* messages" (Issing, 1999b).

1.4   Avoiding excess volatility in inflation, output, and the interest rate

I have so far focused on the level inflation objective. After any shock, however, there are typically different paths which inflation, output, and other relevant economic variables can follow to return to an equilibrium level. This raises an issue of choice of the best possible path, where the optimality ("best") feature must be assessed according to some objective function and typically facing trade-offs between the variability of the different variables.

This topic has been central to academic research on optimal monetary policy for the past three decades, during which the literature has searched for the most efficient way to smooth output and inflation volatility around given equilibrium levels. The rest of this section will briefly review and discuss some of the important contributions of this literature in the context of practical monetary policy strategies.

1.4.1   Credibility redux

Compared with the key problem of how to achieve the level objective, the academic literature has made tremendous progress in analyzing how to avoid excess volatility in inflation, output, and the interest rate.

Without aiming to be exhaustive, I wish to mention three developments. First, identified vector autoregressions (VARs) have uncovered some quantitative evidence on the average functioning of the monetary policy transmission mechanism. In contrast, at the beginning of the 1970s we could mostly rely on ad-hoc lag structures or, more wisely, on Friedman's statement on the long and variable lags of the transmission mechanism.

Second, we now have a better understanding of the general desirable properties of an optimizing approach to monetary policy, in particular a better understanding of the limitations of a purely forward-looking approach. The work by Woodford (2003) has clearly demonstrated that optimal policy should be characterized by history dependence, a characteristic which would bring welfare benefits in a world characterized by forward-looking agents.

Third, new developments based on micro-founded models have shown that, by and large, it is desirable for central banks to adopt a measured response to shocks. In order to avoid large and unnecessary fluctuations in inflation, output, and interest rates, shocks should be offset only gradually, rather than in the shortest possible time.

At the same time, the measured response should not be mistaken for a lenient attitude towards inflation deviations from target. These same models have in fact thrown new light on the benefits of credibility and the precise meaning of commitment. More specifically, it has been shown that the presence of forward-looking variables in the economy generates further benefits from credibility, over and above those related to the inflation bias. Since forward-looking variables react to expected future policy moves, being able to influence expectations of future policy – being credible – has effects on current economic outcomes. This channel of monetary policy transmission operates even if the central bank has preferences that make surprise inflation undesirable.

Clarida, Galí and Gertler (1999) have demonstrated that, in a model where firms cannot adjust their prices continuously, they will set prices depending on future conditions. The so-called New-Keynesian Phillips curve will thus characterize the pricing behavior of firms, that is

$$\pi_t = \beta E_t \pi_{t+1} + \kappa z_t$$

where π_t continues to denote inflation, z_t a notion of output gap, and β and κ are constant parameters. In this environment, a central bank facing an inflationary shock would like to persuade private agents that it is committed to deflation in future periods. The expectation of *future* central bank actions will feed back on current inflation, thus moderating the current impact of the shock on prices. As a result, the central bank will be able to implement a milder *current* policy response than would have been the case under discretion (see lecture 2 for a more detailed discussion of the Clarida, Galí and Gertler model).

This implies that, if the central bank is credible, it will be able to reduce the immediate impact of an inflationary (cost-push) shock simply through the promise of a tough future course of action and, in a sense, irrespective of the impact response.

A credible central bank firmly committed to fight inflation can thus achieve superior outcomes. Since credibility causes a smaller propagation of inflationary shocks, inflation will depart from price stability by less than in the case in which the bank pursues time consistent policies. Consequently, the return to price stability becomes possible through a smaller contraction of aggregate demand, thus with a smaller output loss. It is exactly through an announcement that it cares "little" about output fluctuations that the central bank effectively smooths out the excess volatility of output.

1.4.2   *More on measured vs. aggressive responses*

The benefits of credibility imply that central banks should be relatively aggressive in fighting inflation and deflation. Nevertheless, we have already mentioned that there are also benefits in adopting a measured response to shocks in order to avoid unnecessary volatility in inflation, output, and interest rates. All in all, are there other arguments that would tilt the balance in favor of a lenient response to inflationary shocks and greater concerns for output stabilization?

This question traces back to the debate on the optimal degree of activism of policy during the late 1940s and the 1950s, when it was recognized that reliable information about the long and variable lags in the transmission of monetary policy is typically not available. The corollary was that uncertainty, in the form of limited information on the economy, implies that stabilization policy goals are infeasible. A number of academic economists warned strongly against the implementation of policies that aim at fine-tuning economic activity. Prominent among them was Milton Friedman who, with others, argued in favor of a constant growth rate of money.

Brainard's results mentioned in the Introduction represent a different viewpoint, that is the recommendation for a less aggressive response to shocks in the face of model uncertainty. However, we also mentioned that Brainard's results have proven to be fragile and parameter uncertainty has no general implications for how the response coefficients should be changed (see also Walsh, 2003b). For example, uncertainty about the persistence of the inflation process can lead the policy maker to adjust interest rates more vigorously, so as to reduce uncertainty about the future development of inflation (e.g. Coenen, 2003). A very large degree of interest rate smoothing can in fact generate instability in a model with purely backward-looking structural equations. Smets and Wouters (2002a) discuss the case where the central bank is uncertain about the nature of shocks driving the economy. They consider cost-push shocks, creating a trade-off between price stability and output gap stability, and supply shocks, which do not create such a trade-off. In such a setting they find that assuming all shocks to be supply shocks is the robust policy. Once again, this result warns against pursuing active stabilization policies.

Other recent research has also shown that central banks should moderate the responsiveness of the policy instrument to real activity when underlying data are known to be subject to measurement error (e.g. Orphanides, 2001). The reason is that, when a measurement error occurs, a strong policy response to mismeasured data will induce unnecessary fluctuations in the economy. In fact, the weight given to the individual information variables should depend on how precisely those variables are measured. This is especially applicable to variables such as potential output and the output gap.

All in all, real-world uncertainty about model parameters or, more generally, about model structures is so pervasive and complex that an approach encompassing all cases is very difficult. Judgment must therefore be exercised to assess which approach is most suited at each point in time. Nevertheless, the benefits of credibility, the lack of knowledge on the precise features of the monetary policy transmission mechanism, and the noisy measurement of potential output are all arguments suggesting that policy should be aggressive against inflation deviations from target, but wary of attempting to smooth output fluctuations. This broad conclusion appears to be consistent with the theoretical results on anchoring expectations to the level objective. An aggressive response to inflationary shocks also helps to maintain private sector expectations focused on the price stability objective of the central bank.

1.4.3   The horizon and financial stability

A final viewpoint that has been used to discuss how aggressively a central bank should respond to shocks is that of the policy horizon.[7] Since price stability can be restored more or less quickly after an inflationary or deflationary shock, it has been argued that a quantitative definition of price stability could be accompanied by a specification of the relevant timeframe for the return to price stability. Such a specification would prove useful as a coordinating mechanism for agents' expectations.

A fixed timeframe is certainly sub-optimal, as different policy responses can be appropriate depending on the initial conditions and the source and dimension of the exogenous shocks that cause deviations from the objective. Although the timeframe could be made conditional on the exact type of shock hitting the economy (and this solution has indeed been explored in some countries), an exhaustive classification of shocks is practically infeasible. The already emphasized lack of consensus on the appropriate model of the economy translates here into uncertainty about the appropriate identification of the nature and statistical properties of the shocks.

A recent popular recommendation to deal with this problem is to assign to central banks "target rules" (Svensson, 1999a), rather than simply an objective to pursue. A target rule would be more specific than a simple statement of the objective, as it would also specify, for example, which percentage of any deviations of inflation from target should be closed in each of the time periods following the original shock. In this sense, the target rule would also address the problem of defining the correct horizon for policy.

A target rule would be derived based on a given model to describe the working of the economy and the specification of an objective function for the central bank. In some formulations, only the model of the economy would be required, since the objective function of the central bank would itself be derived optimally in the context of that model. The target rule hence coincides with optimal policy, and the rule-like element of this approach is represented by the central bank's commitment to an inflation target and to an optimizing procedure which has to be employed in the actual pursuit of the target (Svensson, 1999b).

More recently, Giannoni and Woodford (2002a, 2002b) and Svensson and Woodford (2003) have proposed a class of robust, optimal, explicit instrument rules. As well as minimizing the central bank's loss function given the structure of the economy, such rules are robust to residual uncertainty. More specifically, the response to deviations from target of the objective variables does not depend on the properties of the disturbances affecting the economy – such as their variance or serial correlation.

The prescriptions for virtuous central banking embodied in optimizing rules address some of the criticisms of simple rules by avoiding some of the drawbacks associated with a policy reacting mechanically to a specific inflation forecast while encompassing a large information set. However, optimizing rules remain too restrictive in several respects. First, the proposed optimizing procedure seems to underrate the need for judgment in the use and interpretation of any economic model. Second, and more generally, a sequence of policy moves which may be considered optimal on the basis of one model of the economy may turn out to be associated with bad policy outcomes if simulated on the basis of a different model, representing alternative views about the workings of the transmission mechanism.

In this respect, the horizon problem remains unsolved in theoretical research, beyond the pragmatic prescription of a response that achieves a return to price stability over the medium term – rather than immediately. Once again, judgment must be exercised to assess which approach is most suited for a particular shock occurring at a certain point in time.

Recent research has also pointed out the advantages of adopting a forward-looking perspective which extends quite far in the future. This is related, in particular, to the debate on how central banks should accommodate concerns for financial stability. I have argued elsewhere (Issing, 2003a) that this area is plagued by the difficulty of providing an operational definition of financial stability. Nevertheless, in spite of the existence of some conflicting views (e.g. Borio, English and Filardo, 2003; Borio and White, 2003), there seems to be some consensus around the conventional view that price stability and financial stability normally go hand in hand.[8] Inflation is often one of the major factors creating financial instability, for example because it can worsen the asymmetric information problem between lenders and borrowers. The provision of excess liquidity by the central bank and an ensuing abnormal credit growth are factors that can both trigger an inflation outburst and lay the foundations for financial instability.

Thus, concerns about financial stability do not imply that the ultimate objective of monetary policy should not be price stability. Nevertheless, it is conceivable that financial imbalances may sometimes be important enough to possibly constitute a long-run threat to price stability. This highlights the importance of maintaining a sufficiently forward-looking orientation for the horizon, over which the primary objective of price stability should be pursued. In this manner, financial stability would not matter as an objective *per se*, but only to the extent that a potential financial crisis would have adverse longer-term consequences on the maintenance of price stability (see also Bernanke and Gertler, 1999; Gertler, 2003).

At the same time, these arguments illustrate the importance of focusing on monetary and credit developments in order to form a judgment on consumer price inflation in the medium to long run. Such an approach forces a central bank to also consider longer-run developments, rather than focusing on prospective developments just one or two years ahead. This perspective can also highlight risks to price stability stemming from financial imbalances and, at the same time, it is likely to help in avoiding the accumulation of such imbalances.

In this context, simply pursuing an inflation targeting strategy according to an inflation forecast over a one- or two-year horizon is not the optimal policy strategy. The overall costs of inflation might not receive the appropriate weight in a fixed-horizon inflation forecast. At times, strains in the financial system might require that deviations from the inflation objective during shorter periods of time may have to be allowed for, in order to preserve price stability over the medium to long run.

For inflation targeting central banks, this would entail extending the forecast horizon further into the future (e.g. Bean, 2003). This perfectly feasible alternative on theoretical grounds opens up a nightmare scenario when one is confronted with the lack of precision of available forecasts for long horizons. Using US data, Atkeson and Ohanian (2001) argue that one-year-ahead inflation forecasts based on a number of different models, including Phillips-curve based models, cannot beat a forecast based on the random walk. Canova (2002) documents that different models seem to yield better results in different countries and structural models do not tend to dominate more empirically oriented specifications. Obviously, the usefulness of the forecast for inflation forecast targeting strategies does not strictly rely on a successful forecasting performance. Nevertheless, the lack of precision of, for example, three-year-ahead inflation forecasts would in all likelihood make them void of content for communication. The central bank would simply be making conjectures about future scenarios, without a true ability to make an informed assessment on their relative likelihood.

To summarize, an appropriate horizon for the maintenance of price stability can be defined as that which would also implicitly address concerns for financial stability. If the central bank employs a medium-term horizon for the definition of price stability in the context of a strategy encompassing a stability-oriented, forward-looking approach, with due attention paid to money and credit, financial imbalances will implicitly receive the attention they deserve. This is true even if financial stability is not an objective of the central bank and monetary policy aims only at maintaining price stability.

1.4.4   A pragmatic interpretation of theoretical results

A pragmatic way to interpret the relevance of the aforementioned results for practical monetary policy strategies can be given in terms of applied practices. The applied strategies of all major central banks, including the ECB and the Federal Reserve System, tend to incorporate the previously reviewed features of optimal monetary policy to a similar extent.

In particular, all central banks are equally and acutely aware of the multifaceted benefits of credibility and of the importance of ensuring that private sector's expectations remain anchored. All central banks are also fully aware of the existence of policy transmission lags, thus of the needs to adopt a forward-looking, medium-term orientation and to base policy decisions on all relevant information. And no central bank, whether or not adopting inflation targeting, is an "inflation nutter" (in the words of King, 1997).

In the next two sections, I discuss the specific ways in which these general principles have been embodied in the strategies of the Bundesbank and the ECB.

1.5   Pragmatic monetarism: the Bundesbank

In October 1990 I left the university system in which I had spent all my professional life up to that point to become a member of the executive board of the Deutsche Bundesbank. From the first day I was entrusted with the portfolio which had been in the hands of Helmut

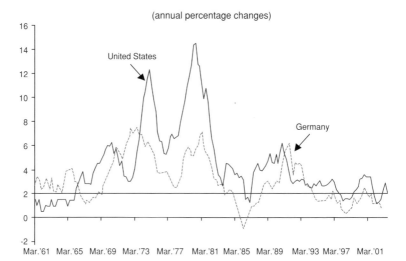

Figure 1.1 CPI inflation, 1961–2001

Schlesinger – at that time vice-president of the bank – for almost twenty years. This implied not only responsibility for the business areas of economics and statistics but also the presentation of economic analysis and monetary policy conclusions to the board and the bi-monthly meetings of the council (the Zentralbankrat), i.e. the highest decision-making body. Responsibility for the *Monthly Report*, the very influential publication of the Bundesbank, was also part of the portfolio.

At that time the Bundesbank was already one of the most respected central banks in the world with a unique track record as an inflation fighter. The Bundesbank had been able to counter inflationary shocks, most of which were international, more effectively than other central banks. German year-on-year inflation never in fact reached double-digit figures in the 1970s. Figure 1.1 shows that Germany experienced a prolonged inflationary shock in those years, but the so-called 'great inflation' that plagued the United States and many other countries never really took hold of Germany.

1.5.1   The framework

Many elements of the approach to monetary policy making outlined in previous sections can be recognized in the Bundesbank's experience with monetary targeting. A firm reliance on the fundamental tenets of monetary economics, on the one hand, and an open-minded approach to dealing with the practical challenges of day-to-day monetary policy making, on the other, represent the foundations of the Bundesbank's approach.

The laws governing the Bundesbank gave it independence and a mandate to "safeguard the stability of the currency." The Bundesbank had been very successful in communicating that this meant safeguarding (only) its "internal stability"; in other words, maintaining price stability.

Under the Bretton Woods regime of fixed exchange rates, the Bundesbank was often confronted with the problem of having to make obligatory interventions in the foreign exchange market. In principle in such a regime the money supply becomes endogenous and domestic inflation is dominated by the international environment. In the early 1970s the problems of the Bretton Woods regime in the context of the "dollar glut" became more and more visible. Finally, the system of fixed exchange rates collapsed. When Germany cut the link to the dollar and moved towards a floating exchange rate, the Bundesbank was freed from its "international bondage." These events coincided more or less with the peak of the "monetarist counterrevolution" (Johnson, 1971).

As the first central bank in the world, in December 1974 the Bundesbank pre-announced a target for the rate of growth of money (8 percent for the central bank money stock in the course of the year). It continued this practice every year until the end of its monetary independence, i.e. until the introduction of the euro.

From the moment the Bundesbank adopted the strategy of monetary targeting there was discussion about to what extent the

Bundesbank had joined the "monetarist camp." Quite often the Bundesbank was simultaneously criticized by monetarists for not sticking to the philosophy of monetary targeting and accused by others of blindly following monetarist orthodoxy. From the German central bank's viewpoint, both sides missed the point. The Bundesbank had never considered accepting the idea of controlling any form of base money or of pursuing monetary targets over the short term. At the same time, Milton Friedman's dictum that in the long run inflation is always a monetary phenomenon and that developments of prices over longer horizons are therefore determined by the expansion of money was always at the centre of its strategy. As already emphasized above, the term "pragmatic monetarism" was sometimes used to describe this position.

In fact, over twenty-four years the Bundesbank adjusted its concept of monetary targeting several times, for example moving to announce target corridors rather than single-figure targets or choosing the broad aggregate M3 instead of the central bank money stock from 1988 onwards. Moreover, the Bundesbank did not base its reactions solely and mechanically on M3 developments. Instead, in addition to M3, it continuously monitored a broad set of monetary, financial and real economic indicators in order to check the information contained in money growth.

The Bundesbank missed its target roughly half the time (see table 1.1). This does not mean, however, that the Bundesbank did not take monetary targets seriously. On the contrary, money growth targets were regarded as constituting the basis for a rule-oriented approach to monetary policy. Announcing a monetary target implied a commitment by the Bundesbank towards the public. Deviations of money growth from the targeted path always had to be justified. Even if it is true that the reputation of the Bundesbank ultimately was achieved by its success in fulfilling its mandate to safeguard the stability of its currency – its ultimate goal – current policy continuously had to be justified in the context of its pre-announced strategy.[9] In this sense,

Table 1.1. *Monetary targets and their implementation (by percentage)*

Year	Target: growth of the central bank money stock or the money stock M3[a]			Actual growth (rounded figures)		Target achieved
	in the course of the year[b]	as an annual average	more precise definition during the year	in the course of the year[b]	as an annual average	
1975	8	–	–	10	–	no
1976	–	8	–	–	9	no
1977	–	8	–	–	9	no
1978	–	8	–	–	11	no
1979	6–9	–	Lower limit	6	–	yes
1980	5–8	–	Lower limit	5	–	yes
1981	4–7	–	Lower half	4	–	yes
1982	4–7	–	Upper half	6	–	yes
1983	4–7	–	Upper half	7	–	yes
1984	4–6	–	–	5	–	yes
1985	3–5	–	–	5	–	yes
1986	3.5–5.5	–	–	8	–	no
1987	3–6	–	–	8	–	no
1988	3–6	–	–	7	–	no
1989	about 5	–	–	5	–	yes
1990	4–6	–	–	6	–	yes
1991[c]	3–5	–	–	5	–	yes
1992	3.5–5.5	–	–	9	–	no
1993	4.5–6.5	–	–	7	–	no
1994	4–6	–	–	6	–	yes
1995	4–6	–	–	2	–	no
1996	4–7	–	–	8	–	no
1997[d]	3.5–6.5	–	–	5	–	yes
1998[d]	3–6	–	–	6	–	yes

Notes:

[a] From 1988: money stock M3.

[b] Between the fourth quarter of the previous year and the fourth quarter of the current year; 1975: December 1974 to December 1975.

[c] In accordance with the adjustment of the monetary target in July 1991.

[d] Embeddded in a two-year orientation for 1997/98 of about 5 percent per year.

Source: Deutsche Bundesbank.

the strategy contributed to the transparency, the accountability, and the credibility of the Bundesbank's policy.

The basic idea of monetary targeting relies on an application of the quantity equation (see p. 34). The strategy requires that the growth of the money stock adjusted for the long-term change in velocity should be in line with potential output growth: $\Delta m = \Delta p + \Delta y - \Delta v$, where Δm is the targeted growth rate of the money stock, Δp the desired price trend (specified "medium-term price norm"), Δy is the estimated growth rate of potential output and Δv is the estimated long-term rate of change in the velocity of circulation of money. The existence of a medium-term relationship between money and prices is simply illustrated in figure 1.2.

The Bundesbank considered its strategy of monetary targeting as a medium-term approach. The derivation of the monetary target took trend variables and normative elements into account. Moreover, short-term deviations of monetary growth from the target never triggered policy measures quasi-automatically (see Issing, 1992).

1.5.2   Monetary targeting at the time of German unification

At the end of the 1980s, the Bundesbank was one of the most respected central banks in the world, with a track record that was almost unique within the central banks of industrialized countries. Up to 1990 monetary targeting as such had proven effective and seemed superior to any alternatives. Would that remain the case following German unification?

Of course, the situation was substantially different from previous years (see also Issing and Tödter, 1995). The introduction of the DM to East Germany on June 1, 1990 prior to political unification on October 3, had made the environment for monetary policy more uncertain. Whereas the introduction of the DM in the former GDR was a logistical masterpiece, the conversion of Ostmark holdings into DMs initially led to an expansion in the money stock which had to be considered as

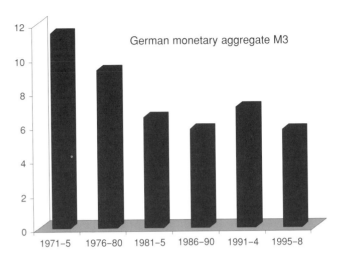

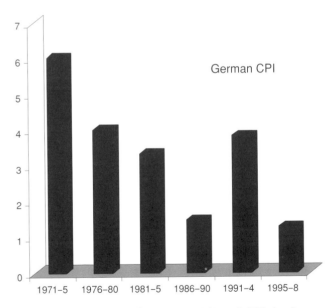

Figure 1.2 Longer-term averages for German M3 and CPI developments (average annual percentage change during the period), 1971–98 (Data before 1991 refer to West Germany)

overly generous. The money supply in East Germany increased by an amount roughly equivalent to 15 percent of the West German money stock (Deutsche Bundesbank, 1990, 1991). However, based on the estimated national product of the former GDR at market prices, an increase of the money supply of only some 10 percent would have been warranted. But this was the result of applying standards from West Germany in the past. Was this appropriate? In deriving its monetary target for 1991 (4–6 percent as in the previous year), the Bundesbank ignored this monetary overhang. As subsequently it could observe a limited reversal in East German demand for money, when households in the new *Länder* geared their portfolios to the longer term, the Zentralbankrat in 1991 – for the first and only time – invoked its power to make a mid-term adjustment and revised the target corridor to 3–5 percent in its mid-year review.

There was much of uncertainty about whether and to what extent the trend of the demand for money in reunited Germany would be different from that in the old Federal Republic. Would reconstruction from scratch require increased monetary support, particularly in view of the East German enterprises' lack of, or at best very inadequate, self-funding? The diverging trends in the individual sectors of the east, especially in the first years after unification, tended to encourage similar considerations, as these suggested a need for increased intermediation by the banking system between lenders and borrowers, a phenomenon known as the "straddle effect" which has been a subject for discussion since the 1960s. One had also to expect that the demand for money might be affected by the dramatic swing in the current account which was running a surplus of over 100 billion DM in 1989 and a deficit of over 30 billion DM in 1991. And, finally, but pointing rather in the opposite direction, there was a marked difference between income and wealth in the east and the west. How should this be taken into account when estimating money demand for the broad aggregate M3, which should also reflect those factors?

Within this environment, could the Bundesbank still assume that the long-term stability of money demand would be unchallenged by

the impact of reunification, and would continuation of monetary targeting remain possible? It was only *ex post* that empirical studies could
show that these disruptions in monetary developments were only of
a temporary nature and did not fundamentally call into question the
monetary targeting strategy (Scharnagl, 1998).

An additional aspect contributed to specific difficulties related to
monetary targeting in reunified Germany. Unification led to a massive
expansionary shock and to high deficits in public budgets. Indeed, the
government sector moved from a balanced position in 1989 to high
deficits, while public sector indebtedness which includes the previous
off-budget funds increased from 41 percent of GDP to 60 percent over
the same time period.

As a consequence inflation in Germany rose quickly. The inflation
rate in West Germany exceeded 4 percent in the second half of 1991
and the first half of 1992 and remained at levels above 2 percent until
early 1994. When setting the monetary targets during this period it was
obvious that inflation would temporarily exceed the normative rate set
so far at 2 percent. The Bundesbank's medium-term-oriented policy
would not aim to bring down the inflation rate by a dramatic restrictive
monetary policy shock but would try in the first place to prevent
inflation from rising unchecked, not allowing financing of second-
round effects of price hikes driven by increases in direct taxation and
bringing down inflation towards the "norm" over the medium term.

How was the bank to preserve credibility for monetary policy in
these circumstances? The first option was, as had already happened
at the beginning of the practice of monetary targeting, to derive the
monetary target based on a rate for "unavoidable inflation" which, in
the circumstances, had to be above 2 percent. On the one hand, the
risk implicit in this approach was that a rate declared "unavoidable"
by the Bundesbank would set a kind of floor to inflation expectations
and influence as such nominal contracts and wages. It also had to
be taken into account that the increase in inflation following German
reunification had been due to demand pressures while in the mid 1970s
and early 1980s oil price shocks had been driving inflation upwards.

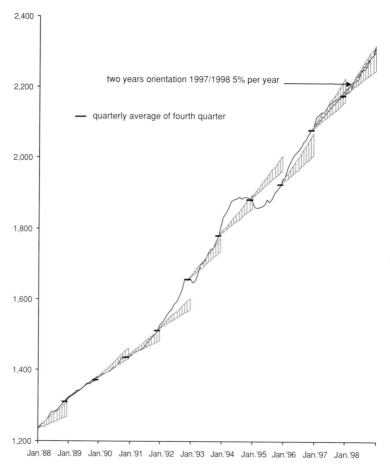

Figure 1.3 M3 in Germany* (average monthly figures in DM billion), 1988–98

Note: * Break-adjusted series. Before 1991, data refer to West Germany. The annual corridors (hatched areas) are derived between the fourth quarter of the previous year and the fourth quarter of the current year.

On the other hand, the advantage of the approach would obviously be that of acknowledging *ex ante* the possibility of temporary increases in the rate of growth of money resulting from the inflationary effects of reunification.

The other option was to stick to the normative rate of 2 percent for inflation in the derivation of the monetary target. Given the orientation of bringing inflation down over a couple of years, this implied that the Bundesbank would be ready, for a short time, to accept a higher rate of monetary expansion than announced in its target. This kind of tolerable, near-future overshooting was obviously inconsistent with a dogmatic interpretation of the monetary targeting strategy. At the same time, however, it would have conveyed the central role of the inflation norm in the strategy and the fact that this was not subject to short-run revisions simply because of the arrival of shocks – not even exceptional ones. This option could therefore be seen as more effective in anchoring expectations at this delicate historical juncture.

The Bundesbank chose the second approach, giving a clear signal that, even in the specific circumstances of German unification, 2 percent remained the norm for inflation. The rate of monetary growth did exceed the target for a while (see figure 1.3), but in its various publications the Bundesbank tried to explain the implications of this approach. In my – certainly partisan, but not necessarily biased – judgment, this decision convinced the public and financial markets of the Bundesbank's unchanged orientation towards price stability. It also contributed to the fact that, in the end, the problem of inflation was overcome better, sooner, and with a smaller output loss than anticipated by most observers.

1.5.3 A number of distortions

By the mid 1990s the problems caused by German unification had been overcome and inflation was on a clear downward trend. Nevertheless, monetary targeting was confronted with a number of new problems. Financial innovation, which up to that point had not caused major difficulties, came about at the same time as shocks arising from changes in taxation. Various tax revisions such as a new withholding tax on interest income triggered shifts between money and other assets or

Figure 1.4 Annual rate of growth of M3 in Germay* (percent), 1988–98
Note: * Break-adjusted series. Before 1991, data refer to West Germany.

disrupted monetary growth through distortions in the demand for credit. The introduction of a split property tax rate contributed to massive portfolio switching at the end of 1994 (see figure 1.4).

Whereas these measures had a substantial impact on monetary developments and contributed to a sequence of years in which the Bundesbank missed its monetary target, they had to be considered mainly as temporary factors and were not to be judged as an argument against the strategy of monetary targeting as such.

The problem posed by the changing composition of money market funds was of a different nature. The monetary content of such funds and their development potential was not easy to assess. At the same time large-scale shifts between euro deposits and domestic money holdings highlighted the substitutive relationship between traditional money holdings and "near-monies." Extending the intermediate target variable to include those assets was an option. On the other hand it would be more difficult to control a monetary aggregate the broader its definition, i.e. including more and more interest-bearing assets. Should the Bundesbank therefore go in the opposite direction and choose a narrower aggregate? In the early 1990s the Bundesbank had conducted studies comparing weighted monetary aggregates with traditional broad aggregates which did not suggest that this would be a promising approach. (Issing, Tödter, Herrmann and Reimers 1993) In the end the Bundesbank decided to retain M3 as its intermediate target variable. At the same time, it amended the extended money stock M3 which had been introduced in 1990 to comprise not only domestic non-bank holdings of deposits with foreign branches and subsidiaries of German banks and short-term bank debt securities but also their certificates of domestic and foreign money market funds. The Bundesbank announced that it would monitor carefully this newly defined extended M3 aggregate, so being prepared for any major shifts in the demand for money.

An interesting aspect in this context is raised by "Goodhart's law," which could be seen to contrast with the positive experience of the Bundesbank targeting money over a long period. In fact, the Bundesbank experience tends to suggest that the law, which states that "any observed statistical regularity will tend to collapse once pressure is placed upon it for control purposes" (Goodhart, 1975, p. 5), depends very much on the behavior of the economic policy authorities. The implied criticism of the Bundesbank's strategy might be challenged by the positive interrelationship between a policy targeting the money supply and stability of money demand. A policy of monetary targeting geared to steadiness and medium-term objectives should reinforce the stability of the monetary relationship and hence the foundation of the policy itself (Issing, 1997).

1.5.4   *The Bundesbank's monetary policy on the way to EMU*

In principle the European monetary system (EMS), was created as a system of equal currencies. De facto the DM soon emerged as the anchor currency. The Bundesbank's monetary policy set the benchmark for the process of disinflation in the 1980s and those currencies which could not, or not fully, keep pace had to devalue.

On July 1, 1990 the European Community entered the first stage of the process leading to European monetary union (EMU). As it happened this event coincided with German reunification which came – in economic terms – as a shock not only to Germany but also to its partners in Europe. The initial impact on the other countries provoked an explosion of exports to Germany. Given the high rate of capacity utilization at that time in West Germany, the strong increase in demand driven mainly by fiscal transfers to the new *Länder* had the consequence of changing Germany's external position overnight; imports ballooned, rising in 1990 and 1991 by 11.5 and 13 percent in real and 9 and 15 percent in nominal terms, respectively.

This positive contribution to GNP – the average figure for EU member countries is almost 0.5 percent in 1990 and 1991 – in a situation of cyclical downturn was highly welcome. This was less true for the tightening of monetary policy that the Bundesbank deemed necessary to counter strong inflationary pressures in Germany. Within the EMS the impact of the Bundesbank's restrictions was immediately transmitted to the other members. Exchange rates came under pressure as these countries were not able to react by adjustment of other macroeconomic variables. Concern about and criticism of German monetary policy was soon being voiced. The argument was that the Bundesbank, as the de facto European Central Bank, should orient its policy not only to the situation in Germany but also with a view to the partner countries. This combined with arguments from inside Germany by several politicians and business leaders to put aside the focus on price stability in the unique historical circumstances until the major challenges of German unification had been overcome.

How did the Bundesbank react under strong pressure from inside and outside the country? The Bundesbank explained that legally it had a clear mandate to preserve the stability of the Deutschmark, a domestic goal. Moreover, it was convinced that it would be wrong to see a contradiction between this orientation and the interests of the European partner countries.

One additional and important aspect supports this view. It was obvious that it would be very difficult to convince the German public of the need to give up the DM for the sake of a single currency in Europe. With the bad experience of their history to draw upon, the people were suspicious of any kind of "monetary reform" and, despite their prevalent European enthusiasm, were extremely reluctant to embrace the project of EMU. Any hint that a "European" orientation might imply less price stability would have been disastrous for the project of monetary union. In the end this might also have undermined the acceptance of the single currency in other countries as people were eager to have not only a common but primarily also a stable new currency.

The German central bank had created a stability culture that set a benchmark. Eventually, all European central banks embraced this culture of stability, the success of which was endorsed when the statute of the ECB was designed in the same spirit as the Bundesbank law, with its major elements of independence and a clear mandate to maintain price stability.

1.6 A stability-oriented strategy: the ECB

How should the ECB deal with the uncertainties created by EMU? From my personal viewpoint, leaving behind the difficulties of coping with unification and its consequences in Germany only meant having to face this more complex question.

The various aspects of uncertainty facing the ECB at the beginning of its life have already been discussed in section 1.2. I will only emphasize here that the interplay of such powerful sources of uncertainty prompted me to state: "never have I felt the impact of uncertainty so acutely as in the weeks that preceded and followed the introduction of the euro and the birth of the single monetary policy" (Issing, 1999a). What were the best policy decisions in such circumstances was by no means obvious.

A key task for the ECB was accurately to gauge the extent to which the successful experience of the Bundesbank's monetary policy should be taken as a reference point.

In June 1992, in a speech at the Paolo Baffi Centre for Monetary and Financial Economics of Bocconi University in Milan, I had stated:

> A central bank's reputation substantially results from its past policy record and its corresponding success in fighting inflation. This reputation provides the basis for the credibility of its current and future work. The European Central Bank is starting out into monetary union from scratch; it has yet to earn a reputation by conducting a sound monetary policy. The European Central Bank can win confidence in this difficult initial phase only by "inheriting," as it were, the tradition of the Bundesbank and other major central banks with a high reputation."

In 1993, at a conference organized by De Nederlandse Bank on "Monetary Policy Strategy in the EMU," I explicitly stated that the ECB should adopt a strategy of monetary targeting. One major argument in favor of this approach was, again, to transfer as far as possible credibility and reputation to the new institution which had to start without a track record of its own.

In the end, when the time came, I did not propose monetary targeting as a strategy for the ECB. While the empirical evidence available in late 1998 suggested that the demand for M3 for a sample of currencies joining EMU was stable and that M3 growth displayed leading indicator properties for inflation, taking such an approach appeared to be very risky – in the end much too risky. Unavoidably, all these econometric studies were based on a period when monetary policy had not been in the hands of a unique institution. Hence, behavioral changes due to a regime shift after the start of Stage Three had to be given high probability. In the same vein, any significant change of the monetary policy strategy, such as a change of the key monetary aggregate soon after the start of monetary union, could have seriously damaged the ECB's credibility. Against this background, there were a number of good reasons to choose a broader-based and more robust monetary policy strategy.

1.6.1   The framework

The ECB's monetary policy strategy is another illustration of a commitment to a procedural framework, which may overcome some of the limitations and risks associated with more narrowly defined monetary policy rules.

First and foremost, the strategy includes a clear commitment to the goal variable, i.e. the primary objective of price stability. In October 1998, the ECB's governing council clarified that price stability would be defined "as year-on-year increase in the Harmonized Index of Consumer Prices (HICP) for the euro area of below 2 percent." In May 2003, after an extensive evaluation of all the characteristics of the strategy, the governing council clarified that, within the definition of price stability, the focus of the ECB monetary policy is to maintain the inflation rate below, but close to, 2 percent. This clarification aims to shed light on the ECB's commitment to maintain a sufficient "safety margin" between the price stability objective and exact zero inflation. The safety margin aims "to guard against the risks of deflation" while also addressing "the issue of the possible presence of a measurement bias in the HICP and the implications of inflation differentials within the euro area."

A fundamental aspect of the definition is that "price stability is to be maintained over the medium term." The medium-term orientation highlights two important general features of the strategy. The first is the choice to adopt a gradual approach in the return to price stability after a shock, hence avoiding any unnecessary volatility in output and interest rates. The second feature is an explicit acknowledgment of the existence of long and variable lags in the monetary policy transmission mechanism: shorter-term-oriented policies would only have the consequence of introducing further noise in the economy.

The strategy also puts forward a robust approach, particularly needed given that it was adopted to cope with the unusually high degree of uncertainty and imperfect knowledge prevailing at the beginning of Stage Three of EMU. This is reflected in the decision to base the assessment of the risks to price stability on the cross-checking of two analytical perspectives, referred to as "two pillars." In turn, the two perspectives are referred to as "economic analysis" and "monetary analysis." Accordingly, the stability-oriented strategy recognizes the need to scrutinize all available information, based on a wide set of economic indicators, in order to improve policy decisions. At the same time, the strategy acknowledges the connection between money and price developments in the medium to long run as one of the most robust known economic relationships.

Naturally, the link between money and prices tends to be stronger over the medium to long term, whereas in the short run several factors may lead to unexpected shifts in the velocity of circulation. A variety of indicators of domestic and international cost and price factors often provide a reasonably accurate account of near-term price developments. Therefore, it seems natural to attribute a more important role to the latter indicators in forming a judgment about short-term price developments, while shifting progressively the emphasis on "money" as the horizon of the assessment lengthens and uncertainty widens.

The two-pillar approach takes advantage of the different time horizons of economic and monetary analyses for the assessment of risks to price stability. The approach provides a framework for cross-checking indications stemming from the shorter-term economic analysis with those from the monetary analysis, which provides information about the medium- to long-term determinants of inflation. This cross-check helps to demonstrate whether the course of monetary policy is broadly pointing in the right direction, thereby ensuring that the economy has a nominal anchor beyond the conventional forecasting horizon.

The similarities between the ECB strategy and the Bundesbank's monetary targeting are obvious. This element of continuity has, in the perception of observers and market participants, enhanced the credibility of the ECB.

At the same time, the ECB strategy is clearly different from monetary targeting. From the very beginning, it was made clear that the "reference value" for the rate of growth of M3 should not be seen as a monetary target. The reference value was in fact immediately announced as a medium-term norm rather than a monetary target for the year ahead (see ECB, 1999; Issing, Gaspar, Angeloni and Tristani, 2001). Since the medium-term trend assumptions underlying the derivation of the reference value for M3 are not expected to change frequently, in May 2003 the ECB announced its decision to discontinue its regular annual review of the reference value.

In spite of these differences with respect to monetary targeting, the ECB strategy has been criticized very early on by academic proponents of inflation targeting for attributing too much importance to money. This line of criticism has been used repeatedly, for example, in the annual "Monitoring the ECB" reports of the CEPR (see www.cepr.org), including the 2004 report on the ECB review of its monetary policy strategy. At the same time, advocates of monetary targeting have accused the ECB of paying too much attention to real variables in its analyses (see the reports prepared by the EMU Monitor group organized by the Zentrum für Europäische Integrazionsforschung of the University of Bonn, www.zei.de). This debate has very soon reached a standstill, in the sense that the arguments used on both sides have remained unchanged over time. From the ECB viewpoint, the simple existence of the debate can be seen as proof that a robust monetary policy strategy was indeed the appropriate choice for the euro area (see Issing et al., 2001, for a more detailed discussion of these criticisms).

Both economic and monetary analyses have been significantly extended and enriched over the first years of life of the ECB, as a result of progress in the production of euro area data and in the development of statistical and analytical tools for the analysis of such data. Rather than entering into detailed descriptions of the various elements that jointly constitute economic and monetary analyses, the rest of this lecture will focus on the role, within these analyses, of two selected indicators: the output gap and M3 growth. These indicators are used as representative examples of the ECB experience with the information coming from two important elements of its monetary policy strategy. In particular, I discuss the degree to which these indicators have provided reliable and useful information in the first years of the monetary union and how they can be expected to continue to play a role in the future. I will then conclude this section with a short, overall assessment of the experience of the single monetary policy so far.

1.6.2   *Economic analysis and the elusive notion of output gap*

As part of its economic analysis for the assessment of future prospects for price stability, the ECB monitors a wide range of economic and financial indicators. The information provided by some of these indicators is summarized in the ECB projection exercises, which are published twice a year. Since the projections are not all-encompassing, however, individual indicators are also analyzed individually.

Amongst these, various "gap" measures are taken into account in internal analyses, consistent with recent theoretical developments. The output gap plays, in fact, a central role in neo-Keynesian models of monetary economics. In simple models, there is a one-to-one relationship between the gap and inflation, and controlling inflation ultimately implies inducing an appropriate level of the gap. In the applied literature, the output gap and capacity utilization measures are also often proposed as useful concepts when trying to understand the current state and prospects for the economy (see, for example, Stock and Watson, 1999). They belong to a wide class of measures that aim to quantify the departures of some variable from a corresponding benchmark value (for example from the respective trend value or, alternatively, from its equilibrium value in the absence of some frictions). Output gap measures of some sort also figure prominently in the literature on monetary policy rules, in particular on Taylor rules (see, for example, Taylor, 1999b).

At the ECB, however, the output gap has never played the fundamental role it possesses in theoretical analyses, for two well-known reasons that diminish its practical usefulness. The first is that the output gap is a latent variable, which is never observed exactly over time. The second is that the gap is, from a theoretical viewpoint, an elusive concept. Its definition is clearly dependent on the model used to define the "equilibrium output" benchmark and various possible benchmarks have been proposed over time. Traditionally, computations of the gap are defined as deviations of actual output from the output level (or growth rate) which would prevail if the economy were at full potential, i.e. exploiting all the available production inputs. Recent monetary models in the new neo-classical synthesis or the New Keynesian tradition, however, tend to emphasize the notion of natural output (Woodford, 2003), in which it is defined as the level of output which would prevail in the absence of nominal distortions in the economy.

Existing evidence based on euro area data shows that different definitions yield substantially different estimates for the gap. While some techniques have been shown to help reduce the measurement error on the output gap estimates (see Camba-Mendez and Rodríguez-Palenzuela, 2003; Rünstler, 2002), the overall degree of uncertainty remains large when model uncertainty is taken into account. Ross and Ubide (2001), for instance, inspect estimates from about fifteen different methods used to estimate the gap. They find large discrepancies and conclude that, "if model uncertainty is taken into account, the gap is a rather uninformative concept."

To summarize, measures of the output gap in real time tend to be fuzzy. The nature of the gap as an unobservable variable makes it impossible to select the best measure on the basis of statistical criteria alone. Theory does not help in the absence of a well-agreed model of the functioning of monetary economies.

Some recent contributions, in fact, propose that the notion of output gap be abandoned altogether, as an unhelpful tool for monetary policy decision making. Walsh (2003a) finds that simple monetary policy rules focusing only on inflation and the *change* in the output gap can, in simple models, outperform inflation targeting. The advantage of these rules is that the change in the gap is subject to less measurement error than the level (e.g. Walsh 2003b). Along similar lines, Orphanides and Williams (2002b) argue in favor of policy rules whereby the change in the monetary policy instrument is a function of the inflation rate and the change in the (unobservable) natural rate of unemployment.

All in all, it seems prudent to look at the results produced by a wide diversity of alternative techniques, but it is difficult to see how the output gap could play in practice the fundamental role that it is sometimes given in theory.

1.6.3   *Monetary analysis and the (mis)behavior of money*

The long-run link between inflation and money growth is a virtually undisputed result in monetary theory. This consensus has been summarized by the present Governor of the Bank of England in his usual illuminating way: "No money, no inflation" (King, 2002). It is equally widely acknowledged, however, that short-run developments of money can be subject to a number of large and persistent (velocity) shocks which blur the long-run link. As a result, in the strategies of many central banks money does play no significant role, at least in external communication. Central banks such as the ECB have instead decided to face the challenge and continue giving prominence to the monitoring of monetary aggregates.

Money growth has had a bumpy ride over the first years of EMU. After remaining above, but close to, the reference value during the first half of 1999, it increased gradually over the second half of the year and created growing concerns of upward inflationary risks from October 1999 onwards.[10] Towards the end of 2000, however, M3 started edging down, while it also became clearer that the measured growth rate was subject to substantial upward distortions due to non-resident holdings of marketable instruments. As of the autumn of 2001, M3 growth picked up again, partly as a result of portfolio shifts away from longer-term financial assets, and it has remained buoyant for some time amidst renewed portfolio shifts.

The analysis of money growth includes the identification of special factors that may affect it. "Special factors" are influences on money or credit that are usually not taken into account in the traditional estimated money demand models for which long and reliable data series are available (see Masuch, Pill and Willeke, 2001).

First, as already mentioned, there were uncertainties about the impact of the start of Stage Three. In January 1999 there was a significant increase in M3 growth driven mainly by the growth of overnight deposits. This movement was interpreted as partly reflecting the effect of portfolio shifts into liquid instruments related to the higher degree of uncertainty experienced at the beginning of the new regime and the change to the new minimum reserve requirements system. An additional factor that might have played a role in the high growth of M3 at the beginning of 1999 was the existence of statistical distortions in the data. Anecdotal evidence suggests that at least part of the increase in the annual rate of growth of M3 in January 1999 was related to statistical factors, such as the introduction of a new reporting scheme or reporting problems linked to the start of Stage Three.

A second, and important, sort of distortion was caused by the inclusion of non-resident holdings of marketable instruments in M3. In the definition of M3 adopted at the start of EMU, all negotiable instruments issued by euro area MFIs (excluding those held by monetary and financial institutions) were included in M3. This decision was taken against the background that the amounts outstanding of these negotiable instruments were rather small before the start of EMU, and were subject to only moderate growth over time. However, since the start of Stage Three negotiable instruments included in M3 grew at a strong pace, driven to a significant extent by demand from investors resident outside the euro area. As a result, M3 growth was increasingly distorted upwards, with the distortion reaching a maximum in the first months of 2001.

Finally, some instances of portfolio rebalancing also appear to have affected the information content of M3. In the first years of EMU, there were two main instances of portfolio shifts. The first was related to one-off portfolio reallocations due to the introduction of the euro and the aforementioned new reserve requirement regime. The second one emerged in the period of financial market instability in the autumn of 2001. The persistent weakness in global stock markets drove investors away from equity and induced a reallocation of portfolios of euro area non-MFI investors towards low-risk assets. This was further enhanced by the rise of uncertainty in financial markets in the wake of the September 11 terrorist attacks. So far, portfolio shifts have been usually interpreted as having a temporary character. The increased liquidity they generate is therefore expected to be reversed in the future and not to generate upward pressure on prices.

This interpretation is partly based on the evidence that long-run money demand in the euro area remains stable, as confirmed by extensive studies based on EU-wide data.[11]

All studies are based on state-of-the-art econometric techniques and address different aspects of the problem of unveiling key features of money demand in Europe.

These studies have certainly not said the final word on money demand stability in Europe. Many topics still await more extensive investigation using rigorous methods, for example the link between liquidity shocks and changes in the level of risk and volatility in financial markets. Our currently available estimates of the interest rate semi-elasticity of money demand are very imprecise (Bruggeman, Donati and Warne, 2003). The leading indicator properties of money also need to be investigated further, even if they have already received some attention within reduced-form models – see Nicoletti-Altimari (2001), Gerlach and Svensson (2003), Trecroci and Vega (2002), Coenen, Levin and Wieland (2003).

By and large, these results confirm that it is difficult to extract information on future price developments from short-run movements in money growth. They also reaffirm, however, the existence of a trend relationship between money and prices, implying that money can play an important role as an indicator of future inflationary pressures in the euro area at medium-term horizons.

The simplest possible way to illustrate such relation is illustrated in figure 1.5, which shows three-year moving averages of money growth and inflation in the euro area.

The figure highlights that the rate of growth of money has indeed been quite consistent with trend inflation over recent years. (The correlation coefficient between the two series is 0.63.) Notably, money growth has tended to anticipate future inflation developments in the euro area. Based on this experience, the recent renewed increases in money growth have to be closely monitored. They represent one

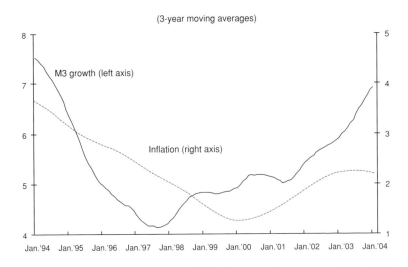

(3-year moving averages)

Figure 1.5 M3 money growth and HICP inflation in the euro area, 1994–2004

important component of the general assessment of the future risks to price stability.

1.6.4   *The experience of the single monetary policy after five years*

As already mentioned above, in 2002 the ECB decided to conduct an evaluation of its monetary policy strategy, the outcome of which was announced on May 8, 2003 (see the background studies collected in Issing, 2003b). An important part of the review was to clarify to the public the aspects of the strategy illustrated in section 1.5.1.

An equally important part of the evaluation, however, was the general assessment of the experience with the implementation of the strategy in the first years of EMU. The evidence accumulated led the ECB's governing council to conclude that the experience with the two-pillar strategy has been successful.

More specifically, the council noted that the strategy, in particular the quantitative definition of price stability, had been very effective in

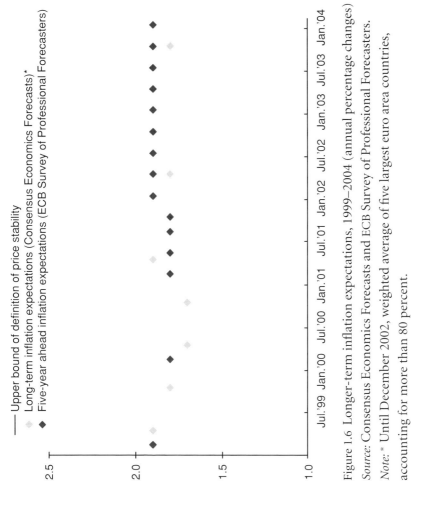

Figure 1.6 Longer-term inflation expectations, 1999–2004 (annual percentage changes)
Source: Consensus Economics Forecasts and ECB Survey of Professional Forecasters.
Note: * Until December 2002, weighted average of five largest euro area countries, accounting for more than 80 percent.

anchoring market expectations. The direct and indirect measures of expected inflation in the euro area have shown a remarkable stability in the last few years, at a level just below 2 percent (see figure 1.6). This is a very important result, perhaps the most important, for a central bank whose mandate is to maintain price stability over the medium term.

Expectations remained anchored in spite of the considerable number and intensity of adverse price shocks that hit the euro area economy in the course of the first years of EMU. Since 1999, economic or financial turbulence has been experienced world-wide via a sequence of oil-price and food-price shocks and dramatic and persistent exchange-rate changes. Amidst such shocks, the ECB used its measured, medium-term-oriented approach, which did allow for some deviation of the inflation rate above the upper bound of the definition of price stability. Nonetheless, there is evidence that such developments in the headline HICP and in short-term inflation expectations left long-term expectations largely uninfluenced – see Gaspar (2003) for a formal test of this hypothesis.

The developments in inflation expectations over these years witness that economic agents understand the medium-term orientation of the ECB's monetary policy and deem it appropriate. The ECB has preserved a degree of monetary and economic stability that would hardly have been conceivable before EMU.

1.7   Conclusions

Theoretical insights and central banking experience are both fundamental components of good monetary policy making, but especially so at the time of historical events.

The Bundesbank's "pragmatic monetarism" was firmly grounded in the monetarist message that inflation is always and everywhere a monetary phenomenon. This implied a "rediscovery" of money and nominal variables, after decades in which prices had often disappeared from economic models. At the same time, the nature of the approach kept the Bundesbank away from a dogmatic and extreme applications of monetarism. As I have argued elsewhere,[12] pragmatic monetarism "constitutes a successful synthesis of a theoretical basis and practical implementation."

Similarly, the ECB's stability-oriented strategy is aware of, and exploits, the advances in monetary policy theory. Partly motivated by the theoretical emphasis on their importance, the ECB does publish its internal projections for future GDP growth and inflation. At the same time, however, the ECB remains skeptical toward the idea that all problems of practical monetary policy making have been solved by the current generation of theoretical models – and toward the conclusion that good monetary policy must invariably coincide with inflation targeting. As in the Bundesbank's case, the ECB approach involves both rule-like features, consistent with the results of monetary theory, and an attention to central banking experience in the implementation phase.

The key messages from monetary policy theory which emerge through the lens of my professional experience can be stated as follows:

Don't try tricks; don't try to be too clever.

Keep steady; remain committed to your mandate even in exceptional circumstances.

Say as much as you can of what you are going to do; announce a strategy.

Don't be dogmatic; instead follow a policy which is always in line with your strategy.

Sound institutional arrangements play a central role. Historical evidence and theory agree in pointing out that central bank independence and a clear mandate for price stability are the basic elements of a sound institutional set-up. They provide the premises to establish credibility, to anchor inflationary expectations and ultimately deliver price stability and foster a stable macroeconomic environment.

We must never forget this message, nor ever take credibility for granted, even at times when price stability is established and there seem to be minor challenges ahead. Credibility is hard to gain, but it is easily lost. To be maintained, it requires continuous vigilance. If lost, it can be regained only at high costs to society.

2

Imperfect knowledge, learning, and conservatism

NATIONAL INSTITUTE OF ECONOMIC AND SOCIAL RESEARCH,
NOVEMBER 10, 2003

2.1 Introduction

Since the 1940s, for more than three decades, culminating in his Nobel Lectures, Milton Friedman critically assessed the contribution of counter-cyclical policy to business-cycle fluctuations.[1] Over the years Milton Friedman asked hard questions: under what conditions will counter-cyclical policy be successful? Do vigorous counter-cyclical actions result in instability? Should long-term goals be given primacy? He also inquired about the limits on obstacles to effective stabilization policy. What are the key factors limiting the feasibility of active stabilization policies? Long and variable lags in the transmission of policies? Endogenous private sector expectations? Policy makers' limited and imperfect knowledge about the structure, current state and prospects for the economy?

It is interesting to recall that when Milton Friedman originally wrote about the effects of stabilization policy, and sought to identify conditions for its success, he did not use an economic model (see Friedman, 1953a). Instead, he resorted to a statistical model, as a device to describe the effects of stabilization policy. Today the tools of stochastic simulation allow us to take a fresh look at the questions raised by Friedman in the context of standard equilibrium models of the economy. Contributions to the literature, led by Athanasios Orphanides and his co-authors[2] are growing fast and include discussion of both conceptual issues and empirical work. All in all these efforts are, in our view, in line with the spirit expressed by Richard Stone in his Nobel Lecture (Stone 1984):

> experience will lead us to reconsider the facts we took into account and our methods for recording and understanding them, the aims we thought desirable, and the controls to be used to achieve those aims. As experience feeds back to modify facts, theories, aims and controls, so the whole picture will change and hopefully we shall get a better model, a better policy and a better plan.

In this lecture we will focus on some selected conceptual issues, using references to empirical evidence as a means to motivation. Friedman's questioning leads naturally to identifying what stabilization policy cannot do. In monetary policy it is at least as important to identify what monetary policy cannot do as it is to identify what it can do. Therefore it is crucial to identify the opportunity set open to policy makers. In other words the theme of this lecture will lead us naturally to discuss the limits to stabilization policies.

Friedman emphasized strongly the role of lagged responses in explaining business-cycle fluctuations. He distinguished a lag between the need for policy action and its recognition – a recognition lag – from a lag between the recognition of the need for action and actual implementation – an implementation lag – and, finally, a lag between policy action and its effects on the economy. The latter is the monetary policy transmission lag that is most often referred to in the literature.[3]

In this lecture we will not consider uncertainty about the transmission mechanism of monetary policy and will disregard policy lags. These assumptions are highly unrealistic but are essential to keep the story simple and manageable. Moreover, if anything they are likely to tilt the environment in favor of active stabilization policies. Indeed, by disregarding policy lags we are able to avoid well-known difficulties associated with economic forecasting.[4] Instead we will focus on issues arising from imperfect knowledge and information, on the part of policy decision makers, and endogenous expectations on the part of the private sector. In more general terms, we will be considering environments where private sector agents and policy makers will have to make inferences about the current state and prospects for the economy. How they do so is key for what follows. Real-time analysis of economic developments is made difficult by pervasive and fast economic change and by imperfect knowledge about the true structure of the economy. The first may be overcome by hindsight. The latter is perennial.

The distinction between fast and widespread economic change and imperfect knowledge should not be exaggerated. Indeed, if the future were conceived as able to change in a completely unrestricted way, then inference and learning would become impossible.

Friedman also highlighted the limits of economic analysis of current economic conditions making a comparison with economic prediction. For example, in 1947, he wrote:

> Serious investigators seeking to establish a chronology of business cycles from past records agree in the main about the movements they regard as cyclical but they differ in not unimportant detail in the dates they set for peaks and troughs. Contemporary interpreters of the course of business have notoriously failed not only to predict the course of business but even to identify the current state of affairs. It is not at all abnormal for some to assert that we in the early stages of deflation and others that we are entering into an inflation.

In this lecture we aim to keep matters as simple as possible. We will sacrifice theoretical generality for the sake of clarity and simplicity. Our examples should be regarded as simple tales intended as metaphors. We will argue that the main features of the story are likely robust to richer frameworks; specifically we will use the simplest model we could come up with. It is in line with the New Classical synthesis and New Keynesian traditions (e.g. Clarida, Galí and Gertler, 1999; Goodfriend and King, 1997, 2001; Goodfriend, 2002). The key ingredient of such a model is a forward-looking Phillips curve where inflation today is determined by expectations of inflation tomorrow and by deviations of output from potential. In other words, inflation is determined by inflation expectations and by the output gap. In this simplest formulation of this model there is a perfect complementarity between price stability and stability of output around potential. The central bank (CB) should ensure price stability and, by doing so, keep output close to potential. As Clarida, Galí and Gertler (1999) – CGG – emphasize, monetary policy in such settings acts to offset demand shocks and to accommodate supply shocks. Since we make the simplifying assumption that there are no policy lags or uncertainty about the transmission mechanism there is no need to consider the aggregate demand relation explicitly. Our assumption implies that the policy maker is always able to offset fully demand shocks completely in line with the CGG prescription.

Unfortunately the set-up described in the previous paragraph is too simple for the purpose of this lecture. There is no trade-off between the maintenance of long-run price stability and the pursuit of an active stabilization policy in the shorter run. One way to extend the model in order to get a policy trade-off between inflation volatility and output gap volatility is to introduce a third type of shock: cost-push shocks. This is done by CGG, who conclude that when cost-push shocks are allowed for, the policy prescription has to be amended only slightly to say that demand shocks should be offset, supply shocks accommodated – as before – and that cost-push shocks imply a trade-off. In CGG's setting, the existence of cost-push shocks justifies the case for conservative central banking à la Rogoff (1985). The result holds for the case where the CB cannot commit to future policies. Rogoff's conservatism story is conceptually very convenient because it allows measurement of an active stabilization policy along a single dimension: the weight of output gap stabilization in the policy maker's loss function. It allows for a simple extension of Friedman's concept of "vigorous counter-cyclical action" to frameworks where policy is conducted in a systematic way. Another very useful tool is Taylor's efficiency frontier showing the trade-off between inflation volatility and output gap volatility (see, for example, Taylor, 1999a). It turns out that Taylor's efficiency frontier provides a very clear graphical device to picture the opportunity set open to policy makers in differing circumstances.

To recapitulate, the lecture will focus on the implications of imperfect information and knowledge on the part of policy makers, and of endogenous private sector expectations for the viability and desirability of an active stabilization policy. The focus will be on imperfect knowledge and information but we will look closely at how it interacts with learning dynamics (endogenous expectations). Our version of Friedman's questions will be as follows:

Given the central bank's difficulties in estimating potential output, might a stabilization policy prove destabilizing?

What implications does uncertainty about the level of potential output have for the inflation output gap volatility trade-off?

What weights on output gap stabilization in the CB's loss function lead to efficient combinations of inflation and output gap volatility? Which weight minimizes society's loss?

How do results change when private sector learning dynamics are considered?

To repeat: in this lecture we will not be striving for generality. Instead we will be using simple numerical examples to illustrate conceptual possibilities. We will argue, in conclusion, that in our view some of the results are likely to continue to be relevant under much more general formulations. Equivalently we will submit that our simple examples are useful metaphors. A rigorous discussion of results in more general settings is, however, far beyond our intended scope here.

The CGG framework will be reviewed in section 2.2. In the text the common theme will be the relation between various environments in which the CB has to conduct policy and the weight that the CB should give to output gap stabilization. The model will be the workhorse used to examine the more interesting cases, from the viewpoint of the lecture, involving learning on the part of the private sector and imperfect knowledge on the part of the CB. In the CGG model the private sector has rational expectations (RE) and the policy maker has perfect information and knowledge about the state and structure of the economy. Section 2.2 will conclude by considering the case where the private sector uses recursive least squares (RLS) to estimate an autoregressive process for inflation instead of RE. We will show that, in the context of a specific example, the weight on output gap stabilization in the policy maker's loss function which minimizes society's loss is the same that obtains under RE. The equilibrium under RLS will be used as a starting point and as a benchmark against which to assess the results presented in the rest of the lecture. In section 2.3 we will make a brief digression to discuss the empirical evidence on the accuracy of real-time output gap estimates. The focus of the section will be on the euro area. In section 2.4 we will discuss the effects of a CB's imperfect knowledge. Specifically, we postulate that the CB cannot directly distinguish between shocks to potential output and cost-push shocks. To enable the CB to do so we endow it with a filtering technique to estimate potential output and thereby the output gap. In this lecture we will consider only a Hodrick–Prescott (HP) filter. We will show, in our example, that imperfect knowledge makes the case for Rogoff's conservatism stronger. The shape of the efficiency frontier will change significantly. More precisely, only combinations of inflation volatility and output gap volatility corresponding to low weights on output gap stabilization will be efficient. In section 2.4 we will also consider the interaction between a CB's limited knowledge (and information) and learning dynamics. We will show that, in our example, the introduction of learning on the part of the private sector leaves the case for conservatism basically unchanged. The qualitative characteristics of the inflation output gap volatility trade-off will stay the same as before. However, inflation volatility will increase much faster as a function of the weight on output gap stabilization. In section 2.5 we will consider how robust our results are to different assumptions on the accuracy of the CB's knowledge and information. In this section we will return to our benchmark case of private sector learning on the basis of RLS. This will be the only case considered. A simple modeling device will enable us to consider a continuum of cases between the extremes of observable cost-push and potential output shocks – the perfect information case of section 2.2 – and CB's inference on the basis of the HP filter – the imperfect knowledge case of section 2.4. A number of interesting conclusions follow. First, as expected, society's loss increases and the policy maker's opportunity set shrinks as knowledge about the economy deteriorates. Second, under the same conditions, and again as expected, the case for conservatism becomes stronger. Third, the relations between the degree of activism of the CB and the volatility of inflation and of the output gap change parametrically with the quality of available knowledge. The most remarkable feature is that the *shape* of the relations changes. In section 2.6 we will conclude.

2.2 Time inconsistency, cost-push shocks and Rogoff's conservatism

Our starting point will be provided by a set-up where there is a time inconsistency problem associated with output gap stabilization in the face of cost-push shocks.[5] The time inconsistency problem remains in spite of the fact that the CB is not trying to push output above potential, thereby avoiding inflation bias (Kydland and Prescott, 1977; Barro and Gordon, 1983a, 1983b). Clarida, Galí and Gertler (1999) show that even in the absence of inflation bias, time consistency remains a problem in the context of a simple New Keynesian model of the economy when we allow for cost-push shocks.

The fundamental equation that we will be using is the simple New Keynesian Phillips curve:

$$\pi_t = \beta E_t \pi_{t+1} + \kappa(y_t - \bar{y}_t) + u_t \qquad (2.1)$$

where π_t denotes the inflation rate, E_t the expectation objector, y_t denotes real output, $\bar{y}_t$ potential output which coincides with the ideal level of output from the viewpoint of the CB, and, finally, u_t a cost-push variable that affects inflation without affecting the target level of output. We will make the simplifying assumption that the discount factor β equals one in the remainder of the lecture. This equation can be justified from the (log-linearized) optimal pricing decision of a monopolistic producer faced with sticky prices à la Calvo and we refer to Woodford (2003) for a complete derivation. The "cost-push" shock, not present in the Woodford exposition, can be motivated by a time-varying elasticity of substitution in consumption between the goods produced in the economy. Changes in the elasticity of substitution across goods allow for a change in the monopolistic competition mark-up. With such an interpretation, Steinson (2003) derives equation (2.1). Furthermore,

$$u_t = \rho_u u_{t-1} + \upsilon_t \qquad (2.2)$$

$$\bar{y}_t = y^* + \varepsilon_t \qquad (2.3)$$

$$\varepsilon_t = \rho_\varepsilon \varepsilon_{t-1} + \omega_t \qquad (2.4)$$

where υ_t and ω_t are white noise processes with variances σ_v^2 and σ_w^2, respectively. In the simulation part of what follows we will assume that the persistence of the cost-push shocks is 0.3 and that of potential output 0.9, reflecting the idea that potential is driven by highly inertial processes such as technology shocks. Furthermore, we use $\kappa = 0.2$. For the rest of this section, the stochastic process generating potential output plays no role. Therefore we will rewrite equation (2.1) in order to eliminate it. However, the specification making the influence of the path of potential output explicit will be key for our formulation of the CB's problem in the case of imperfect knowledge (see section 2.4 below), and therefore deserves discussion.

Potential output can, and indeed has, been defined in a number of different ways (see also section 2.3 below). In empirical work, the gap has been defined as the deviation from a linear or cubic trend. Alternatively, a filter such as the HP can be employed to single out business-cycle frequencies. In the theoretical ad hoc macroeconomic models of the 1970s and early 1980s the focus was on the gap concept and it was typically specified as a link between the gap and inflation. Next, it was assumed that the CB cared about both inflation and the output gap and optimal policy could then be studied. Hence there was no need to provide an accurate description of what notion of potential was used, apart from the conclusion that a closed gap was consistent with steady-state inflation.

More recently, the use of micro-founded models widened the range of possible concepts. One of the principal achievements of Woodford in a series of papers culminating in his seminal textbook (Woodford, 2003) was to bridge the gap between the micro-founded literature and policy practice. In particular, Woodford shows how to derive not only the structural link between inflation and output, but also the loss function used by, for example, Rogoff (1985) in his analysis of the conservative central banker (i.e. quadratic in inflation and output). In that exercise the notion of the output gap is crucial. Woodford shows that the one (to a second-order approximation) consistent with the quadratic criterion is when potential is defined to be efficient, which in the simple model equates to the equilibrium at which prices are flexible (as opposed to the sticky ones assumed to prevail in the actual economy). With this interpretation, the empirical economist/policy maker is faced with an intricate problem in that the output gap is model-dependent. Faced with a wide selection of models emphasizing various sources of inefficiencies that monetary policy according to the theory could alleviate, the policy maker is also faced with an equal plenitude of output gap estimates. An important point is that this uncertainty can prevail also *ex post* if the policy maker wears the wrong spectacles (relative to the truth) when revisiting history. We offer an admittedly crude way to capture this below, by assuming that the central bank uses an HP filter to extract potential output, and can only observe the mix of the inflation and potential output shock. Furthermore, we will assume that potential output is relatively variable, as is the case in these models since the flex-price equilibrium is driven by a number of shocks in the fully fledged models. In particular, we will assume that the variance of potential output shocks is 0.9 and the variability of cost-push shocks is 0.6. Besides providing a justification of the loss function previously used, the micro-founded approach furthermore gives a welfare-based weight on the output gap. In the ad-hoc analysis, the weight describing social preference simply had to be assumed to be a particular value, without a model-consistent motivation. From a conceptual viewpoint, this placed no constraint on the analysis of Rogoff (1985), since his point holds for all values of the true weight. However, when creating illustrative examples below, we have to take a stand on a value. In the fully rigorous case, this weight is a function of the micro-founded parameters. We use a relative weight, λ^t, of 0.1 as representing the approximated welfare function, a value in line with what comes out of micro-founded derivations.

Before we proceed to eliminate the explicit dependence of inflation on potential output, in our first illustration of the simple model with observable potential, it is useful to interpret the nature of potential output shocks versus cost-push shocks.

Several remarks are in order. First, cost-push shocks are normally conceived as deriving from time-varying mark-ups in goods and labor markets, and on time-varying taxes on factor incomes or on sales of goods and services. In contrast, shocks to potential output come from changes in technology or preferences. However, if the policy maker were to observe only the combination between inflation and output, he would see a linear combination between the shock to potential output and the cost-push shock. He would not be able to distinguish

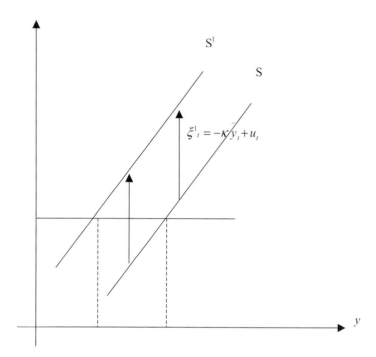

Figure 2.1 Informational assumptions

directly between these two shocks (see figure 2.1). Second, we write the loss function of the CB as

$$L = (1 - \beta)E \sum_{i=0}^{\infty} \beta^i \left((\pi_{t+i} - \overline{\pi})^2 + \lambda (z_{t+i})^2 \right) \quad (2.5)$$

and focus on the limit when β (the discount factor) goes to 1 and where z_t denotes the output gap, that is

$$z_t = y_t - \overline{y}_t$$

The definition of the output gap makes it clear that a positive cost-push is equivalent to a negative shock to potential output of suitable magnitude (specifically $1/\kappa$ times as large). The only difference is normative. The latter shocks affect the target level of output while the former do not. If we allowed cost-push shocks to affect the target level of output, there would be a perfect complement between price stability and output gap stabilization.

Let us now redefine the output gap as:

$$z_t^n = y_t - y_t^n = y_t - \overline{y}_t + \frac{1}{\kappa} u_t$$

$$= y_t - y^* - \varepsilon_t + \frac{1}{\kappa} u_t$$

where $\varepsilon_t - \frac{1}{\kappa} u_t = -\frac{\xi}{\kappa}$ may simply be interpreted as a supply shock (the horizontal shift of the supply curve in figure 2.1). If we were to use z_t^m as the definition of the output gap there would be no trade-off.[6]

Rewriting equation (2.1) using the definition of the output gap z_t we obtain:

$$\pi_t = E_t(\pi_{t+1}) + \kappa z_t + u_t \tag{2.1a}$$

where we have made use of the simplifying assumption that $\beta = 1$. The time-consistent solution to the problem of the CB, optimizing (2.5) every period subject to (2.1a), leads to the well-known linear trade off in the presence of cost-push shocks[7]

$$z_t = -\frac{\kappa}{\lambda}(\pi_t - \overline{\pi}) \tag{2.6}$$

Furthermore, it is possible to use the linear trade-off relationship, the Phillips curve, and the definition of the output gap to write the output gap and deviations of inflation from target as explicit functions of the cost-push shock:

$$z_t = -\frac{\kappa}{\kappa^2 + \lambda(1 - \rho)} u_t \tag{2.7}$$

$$\pi_t - \overline{\pi} = \frac{\lambda}{\kappa^2 + (1 - \rho)} u_t \tag{2.8}$$

Equation (2.8) makes clear that the volatility of inflation around target depends on the weight on output gap volatility in the CB's loss function. Specifically, if this weight were zero, then inflation volatility would disappear as inflation would always be equal to target. In contrast, output volatility would be relatively large. By varying the weight λ it is possible to trace a trade-off between inflation volatility and output gap volatility (see, for example, Taylor, 1999a).

Figure 2.2 shows an example of the relation between the variance of inflation and the variance of the output gap, on the one hand, and the weight on output gap stabilization, on the other. We also show the efficiency frontier, that is the relation between the variance of inflation and the variance of the output gap. The figure has four quadrants. The first quadrant, top right, displays the relation between the volatility of inflation and the volatility of the output gap. In other words, it shows Taylor's efficiency frontier. The efficiency frontier can be derived by using the relationship between the weight on output gap stabilization in the central banker's loss function, λ, on the one hand, and inflation volatility (top left quadrant) and output gap volatility (bottom right quadrant), on the other. The bottom left quadrant contains an auxiliary 45-degree line, corresponding to the λ axis. Figure 2.2 makes clear that there is a convex trade-off between the volatility of inflation and the volatility of the output gap. In figure 2.3 we plot society's loss as a function of the weight on output gap stabilization in the CB's loss function.

Figure 2.3 shows, following Clarida, Galí and Gertler (1999), that society is actually better off delegating monetary policy to a central bank that underweights output gap stabilization relative to society's true weight. The optimal weight that society would wish to delegate to the CB, λ^d, can be written as a fraction of the true weight in society's loss function:

$$\lambda^d = (1 - \rho_u)\lambda^t \qquad (2.9)$$

where λ^t denotes the weight on output gap stabilization in society's loss function. The CB endowed with λ^d will deliver more output gap volatility and less inflation volatility than the CB whose loss coincides with society's. In figures 2.2 and 2.3 $\lambda^t = 0.1$, $\rho_u = 0.3$ and therefore

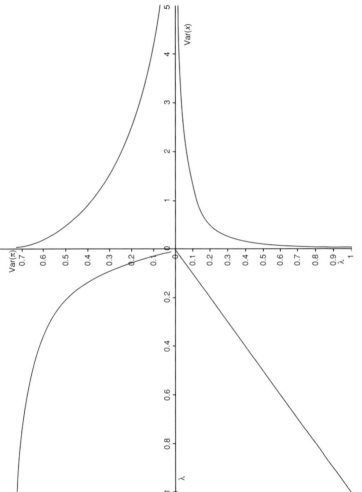

Figure 2.2 Rational expectations, observable shocks

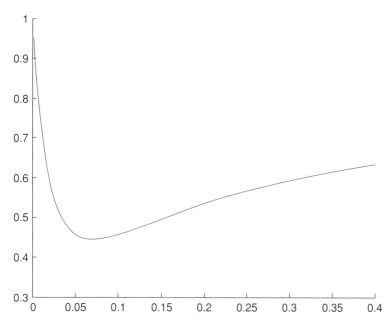

Figure 2.3 Loss: rational expectations with observable shocks

$\lambda^d = 0.07$. What is the intuition for this result? First, it is important to note that if cost-push shocks are stationary there is no systematic inflation level bias. Second, nevertheless, the optimal time-consistent policy departs from optimal policy under commitment. If the CB could commit to the future policy action it would, in the presence of a persistent cost-push shock, like to promise to contract output in the future in order to stabilize inflation and inflation expectations and to spread the costs associated with the cost-push trade-off over time. Private sector agents, however, will realize that the CB has an *ex post* incentive to renege on its promises. A reduced emphasis on output gap stabilization can be interpreted as a second-best solution to this problem. It is, however, important to notice the shape of the loss function under rational expectations and observable shocks. It is clear from figure 2.3 that the loss increases steeply to the left-hand side of the optimal λ, while it increases gradually to its right-hand side. In other words, under the assumptions made, deviations in the direction of excessive conservatism entail larger losses than the converse.

It is opportune here to make a short detour. Alan Blinder, in his Lionel Robbins Lecture (1998) contrasts the old and new debate on rules versus discretion. He contrasts the earlier literature in the Friedman tradition with a newer tradition based on Kydland and Prescott (1977) and Barro and Gordon (1983a, 1983b). He is skeptical about Friedman's argument and doubts whether the inflation bias result can be seen as a realistic representation of central bank practice. He argues that central bankers do not try to push output above potential because they know that would not be sustainable and that it would eventually lead to inflation. In our set-up his criticism does not hold. Since the CB is trying to stabilize output around potential there is no systematic inflation bias.

Before looking at the case of policy makers' imperfect knowledge of the true model of the economy it is worthwhile taking another detour to look at departures from rational expectations. In this section we will consider the case where private sector expectations are endogenous through a learning mechanism. Under rational expectations the inflation process can be written as:

$$\pi_t^{RZ} = (1 - \rho)\overline{\pi} + \rho\pi_{t-1}^{RE} + \frac{\gamma}{1 - \gamma\rho}\upsilon_t \qquad (2.10)$$

where $\gamma = \lambda/(\kappa^2 + \lambda)$. Therefore, it is not unreasonable to postulate (following Orphanides and Williams, 2003b, and Gaspar and Smets, 2002) that private sector agents form these expectations after estimating a simple autoregressive process for inflation as in:

$$\pi_t = c_{0,t} + c_{1,t}\pi_{t-1} + \eta_t \qquad (2.11)$$

We will consider in this section that the private sector estimates (2.11) using RLS. The assumption implies that the private sector has an infinite memory. The private sector never forgets. The process generating private sector expectations is the only difference relative to CGG. Specifically we still assume that the CB observes the true state of the economy and operates in full knowledge of the economy's structure. Under these assumptions the situation looks entirely analogous to that obtained under RE, except for one thing. We will assume that the private sector observes only lagged information. In concrete terms in period t only information up to $t - 1$ is available to the private sector. This is a simplifying assumption made in order to avoid the simultaneity problem that might otherwise surface since current inflation is not pinned down until expectations are set. Restricting the information set of the private sector in this way weakens the case for a conservative central banker under rational expectations. In this case, the optimal weight on the output gap is around 0.09.[8] The intuition is that when the information set is lagged by one period the response of private sector expectations to cost-push shocks diminishes.

Figure 2.4 shows the four-quadrant chart for the RLS case. In figure 2.5, the solid line shows the optimal weight on output gap stabilization for λ^d equal to 0.1 and the result is around 0.085.

The case of private sector RLS learning will be systematically used as a benchmark in what follows.

Some remarks concerning the foregoing are in order before concluding this section. First, the environment in which the policy maker has to operate is very favorable. The policy maker knows the true structure of the economy and observes the relevant shocks. The only limitations assumed relate to the endogeneity of private sector expectations and the inability to commit to a future course of policy. Second, although there is a case for a conservative CB à la Rogoff, it is clear from figure 2.3 that the loss to society is very flat to the right of λ^d meaning that the opportunity cost of appointing a less conservative CB does not increase rapidly. In contrast, to the left of λ^d the opportunity cost of conservatism increases rapidly.

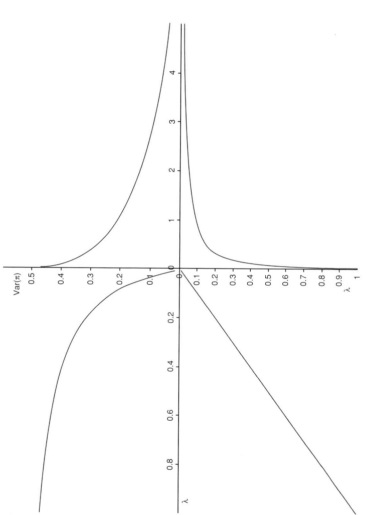

Figure 2.4 Private sector learning; central bank has perfect information

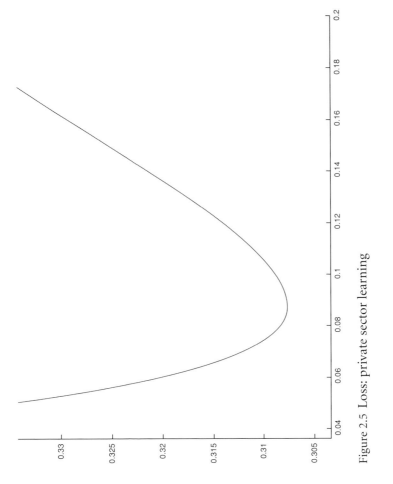

Figure 2.5 Loss: private sector learning

2.3   Empirical output gap uncertainty[9]

We aim to extend the analysis in the previous section to a situation where the central bank does not observe the output gap directly. To motivate this, we start by reviewing some empirical evidence. A number of authors have shown that real-time estimates of the output gap are unreliable. Orphanides (2001), Orphanides and van Norden (2002) and Nelson and Nikolov (2001), the first two for the US, the last for the UK, find that revisions to initial releases of output gap estimates are large. Therefore they infer that the respective confidence intervals must be large. Orphanides and van Norden (2002) examine output gap estimates from univariate detrending methods. They find that revisions in real-time estimates are of the same order of magnitude as the output gap estimates themselves. One obvious limitation associated with reliance on univariate methods stems from the fact that policy-making institutions rely on large information sets when assessing the current state and prospects for the economy. However, Orphanides (2001), using historical estimates produced by the Federal Reserve Board, finds a pattern of revisions over time similar to Orphanides and van Norden. Nelson and Nikolov report similar findings for the UK on the basis of official time series from the Treasury. These findings are highly relevant for policy. Orphanides (2001), for instance, argues that if only the "correct" *ex post* measure of inflation of the output gap had been available in real time, the conduct of monetary policy, following a standard Taylor rule would have been able to prevent the "great inflation."

Figure 2.6 shows some features of real-time estimates of the euro area output gap. It shows five different univariate and multivariate methods, including the HP filter and four multivariate unobserved components methods, taken from Rünstler (2002). Model P is the time-varying parameter gap model (proposed by Gordon, 1997), which relies on a standard aggregate supply curve where current inflation depends on expectations of current inflation and on the output gap.

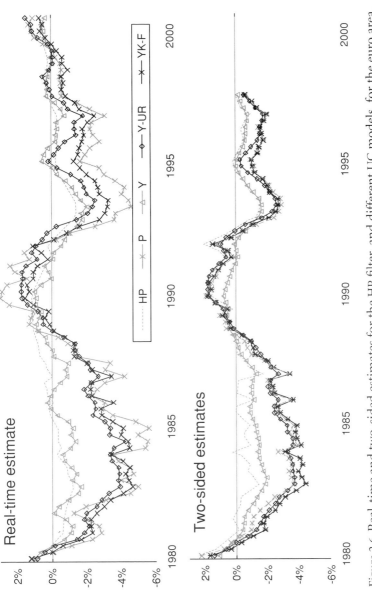

Figure 2.6 Real-time and two-sided estimates for the HP filter, and different UC models, for the euro area, 1980–2000

Model Y adds a decomposition of output into trend and cycle to model P. Models YK-F and Y-UR build on model Y by adding, respectively, total factor productivity and the unemployment rate (see Rünstler, 2002, for further details). Analogously to the above reported findings the difference between the various real-time estimates are large. Visual inspection shows that the differences between two-sided estimates are significantly smaller.

Recent work by ECB staff (Camba-Mendez and Rodríguez-Palenzuela, 2001, and Rünstler, 2002) argues that uncertainty is substantially reduced when multivariate models are used. The intuition is that multivariate approaches make use of information contained in the co-movements of output with other series (e.g. productivity, employment or capacity utilization). Research is currently ongoing to reconcile what seem to be different judgments about the precision of multivariate output gap estimates based on the claims of Orphanides (2001) and Nelson and Nikolov (2001), on the one hand, and Camba-Mendez and Rodríguez-Palenzuela (2001) and Rünstler (2002), on the other.

Whatever the case may be, our interest here lies in the much deeper source of uncertainty arising from the possibility of model misspecification. Ross and Ubide (2001), for example, look at estimates of output gaps for the euro area produced by fifteen different methods. They find large differences and, therefore conclude that, "if model uncertainty is taken into account, the gap is a rather uninformative concept." Indeed, the output gap is an elusive concept even at the theoretical level. It is defined as the deviation of output or economic activity from some reference benchmark and is clearly dependent on the definition of the benchmark. Alternative definitions are, of course, possible, the more so given the lack of professional agreement in the profession concerning which model best captures the short- to medium-term dynamics of the economy. However, as we have argued before, models in the New Classical Synthesis or New Keynesian tradition (see, for example, Goodfriend and King 1997, 2001; Clarida, Galí

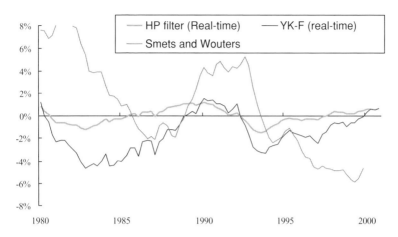

Figure 2.7 Empirical properties of different estimates, euro area data, 1980–2000

and Gertler, 1999; Woodford, 2003) are becoming the reference for the discussion of monetary policy. One outstanding example within the class of stochastic dynamic general equilibrium (SDGE) models with enough structure and detail for empirical implementation is Smets and Wouters (2002b). Unfortunately, output gap measures based on such models do not look at all like measures produced relying on standard univariate or multivariate methodologies such as the ones referred to above. Figure 2.7 illustrates differences in estimates obtained when different concepts are used. It is remarkable to see that, not only are there sizeable differences between the measure of the gap obtained from Smets and Wouters (2002b) relative to the other measures, but even the sign of the estimated gap is opposite for extended periods of time.

Here it is this latter case that we try to capture. We assume that potential output is volatile, in line with the definition of potential compatible with SDGE models. The CB, however, assumes instead that potential output behaves smoothly over time. Starting in the following section we discuss the limits this sort of imperfect knowledge imposes on active stabilization policies.

2.4   Output gap uncertainty, learning, and conservatism

As in section 2.2, we will assume that private sector agents observe inflation up to the previous period, estimate the autoregressive process for inflation and make forecasts for future inflation (two-step ahead). The novelty is that we will now relax the assumption of perfect knowledge on the part of the policy maker. There are two main ideas that we use in order to make the approach operational. First, we assume (see figure 2.1) that the CB observes the private sector's inflation expectations and the combined price-persistent shock (cost-push minus κ times the shock to potential output: $\xi_t = u_t - \kappa \varepsilon_t$). We further assume that the CB is endowed with a HP that it uses to estimate potential output. Second, the CB does not know the true structure of the economy. Instead the CB conducts its policies on the basis of a number of simple heuristic principles: (a) it aims to offset demand shocks; (b) it seeks to accommodate potential output shocks; and (c) it strives to manage cost-push shocks in line with a linear trade-off. The stronger the emphasis on output gap stabilization the greater the rise in inflation that the CB allows for in response to a positive cost-push shock. We assume further that the CB observes private sector expectations before setting policy.

Bringing the two assumptions above together requires a further assumption. Specifically, what does the CB assume about κ? We assume that the CB implicitly uses the 'true' value of κ when making inferences about the cost-push shock, from its estimate of potential and when managing the linear trade-off. We finally assume that the CB makes no further use of this value.

It is interesting to note that, in this model, when the CB finds an unexpected increase in inflation it will interpret it as caused by a cost-push shock. If the CB estimates the potential output will diverge from the true path of potential output, the behavior of derived cost-push shocks becomes the dominant 'explanation' for current inflation.

In order to be able to identify the importance of various factors at play we will introduce imperfect knowledge in the model, step-by-step, as follows. First, we will assume that the coefficients in the autoregressive process used by the private sector to forecast inflation are fixed. Specifically, we will take the coefficients that we have obtained in the simulations shown for the RLS algorithm at the end of section 2.2. Secondly, we will consider the case of RLS learning. Finally, we will consider the results for the case of constant-gains learning for different estimation windows.

Imperfect knowledge significantly changes the results presented before, even for the case when the parameters in the inflation autoregressive process that the private sector uses to forecast inflation are kept fixed. The results are plotted in figures 2.8 and 2.9. It is interesting to note that the shape of the relation between inflation volatility and λ, plotted in the second quadrant of figure 2.6, stays the same. In the case of exogenous parameters in the autoregressive process used to generate private sector inflation forecasts, the relation shifts up, but not by much, and the concave shape of the relation is preserved.

However, the same does not hold true for the relationship between λ and the volatility of the output. The relationship is shown in the fourth quadrant (bottom right) of figure 2.8. In fact the relationship is no longer monotonic. Moreover, the degree of feasible volatility increases very significantly. The relationship has moved significantly to the right. The first result is more significant from an economic point of view. Examining the relationship more closely one sees that if policy is conducted by a CB with a λ higher than 0.1, volatility of the output gap starts to increase. In this range volatility of inflation and the output gap both increase with λ at the same time. This corresponds to the positively sloped section of the frontier in the first quadrant. The frontier has bent backwards. The points in the positively sloped portion of the frontier are not efficient. It is possible reduce volatility of inflation and of the output gap simultaneously. Now the set of

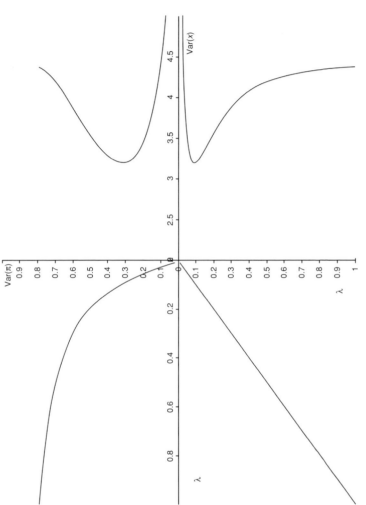

Figure 2.8 Central bank imperfect information, private sector with fixed RLS coefficients

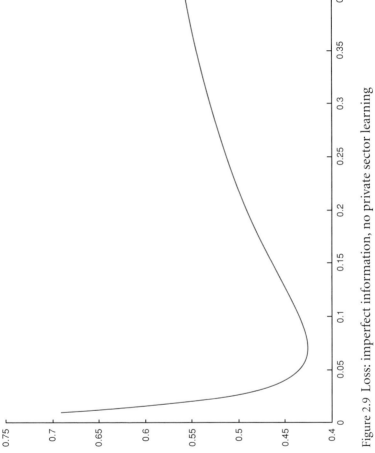

Figure 2.9 Loss: imperfect information, no private sector learning

efficient points – those for which it is impossible to reduce the volatility of inflation and the volatility of the output gap at the same time – corresponds to a range of λ in a narrow range close to zero. Visual inspection suggests a range from zero to about 0.1. Higher values of λ lead to dominated combinations of volatility. In other words, figure 2.8, directly illustrates Friedman's idea that in the presence of imperfect knowledge a strong emphasis on stabilization may prove destabilizing. The highest efficient value of λ is precisely the value that leads to the minimum feasible output gap volatility.

The shift in the relationship between output gap volatility (and inflation) and λ, and the fact that the first is no longer monotonic, implies that the weight on stabilization that minimizes society's loss falls relative to our benchmark case. Additionally, the flat nature of the loss function disappears and the loss becomes much more symmetrical around the optimal weight.

We interpret the results in figures 2.8 and 2.9 as entirely analogous to Rogoff's (1985) case for a conservative central banker. In Rogoff's setting the idea was that in the presence of a labor-market distortion leading to an inflation-bias society was better off with a central bank that placed less weight than society on output stability. The optimal weight was shown by Rogoff to be lower than society's weight, but greater than zero. The story is different in our setting. Here there is no problem of inflation-level bias. Our results are driven by the assumption that the central bank does not observe potential output. It has to estimate it on the basis of a standard filtering technique. Under this assumption, and given the rest of our model, the set of efficient combinations of inflation volatility and output gap volatility corresponds to weights on output gap stabilization lower than society's, including zero. Only conservative central bankers are efficient. Moreover, as in Rogoff (1985), the optimal delegation weight from society's viewpoint is lower than society's but greater than zero.

The results are further strengthened (but not qualitatively changed) when we allow for endogenous learning (see figures 2.10 and 2.11).

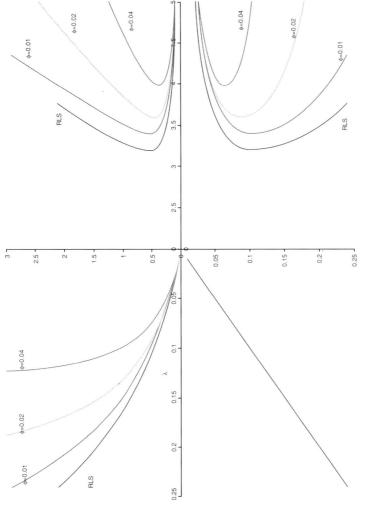

Figure 2.10 Constant gain: learning and imperfect information

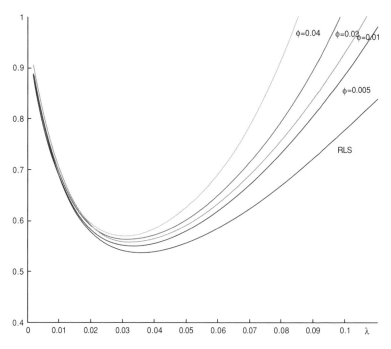

Figure 2.11 Losses with output gap uncertainty and private sector learning

Let us start by considering the case of RLS learning. The difference relative to the previous case is that now the private sector is updating its estimates of the parameters in its autoregressive equation for inflation (equation (2.11)) in line with its RLS algorithm. The results in the first and the fourth quadrant of figure 2.10 seem similar to those in figure 2.8. Apparently the shapes of the curves have not significantly changed. The frontier bends back as before and the set of efficient points corresponds to λs in a range close to zero. Moreover, it holds true again that the maximum efficient value of λ is still at the level that minimizes the volatility of the output gap. It is important, however, to realize that the relation between active stabilization policy and inflation volatility in the second quadrant has now changed shape. Not only has it shifted up, but the relation has turned from concave to convex.

Convexity means that inflation volatility now rises increasingly quickly as a function of emphasis on output stabilization. This explains the U-shaped relation between society's loss and the policy maker's weight on output gap stabilization.

Let us now consider the case where private sector agents estimate (2.11), using constant-gain least squares learning algorithm à la Evans and Honkapohja (2001). Specifically:

$$c_t = c_{t-1} + \phi R_t^{-1} x_{t-1} (y_t - x_{t-1}' c_{t-1}) \qquad (2.12)$$
$$R_t = R_{t-1} + \phi(x_{t-1} x_{t-1}' - R_{t-1})$$
$$y_t = \pi_{t-1}, \quad x_t = [1 \ \pi_{t-1}]'$$

where ϕ is a constant gains parameter which implies that observations from past periods receive a declining weight as time goes by. This is a rule-of-thumb relationship between the constant gain parameter and the length of the estimation window as in ($\phi \cong \bullet /l$) where l denotes the length of the data sample. In the case $\phi \to 0$ we approach the case of recursive least squares with infinite memory, provided that the initial conditions for the parameters are set according to the RLS equilibrium.

As before, in period t, agents have observations up to $t - 1$, and they make their forecasts for future inflation. Therefore they have to produce two-step-ahead forecasts.

In figures 2.10 and 2.11, we show the results for the case where $\phi = 0.005; \phi = 0.01; \phi = 0.02$ and $\phi = 0.04$. Orphanides and Williams (2003a) argue that a ϕ in the range from 0.01 to 0.04 is likely to allow the learning algorithm to replicate the data available data on expectations.

It is clear that in the case of constant gains learning, for the relevant parameter range, inflation volatility increases much more rapidly in response to increased emphasis on output gap stabilization than under RLS. The variance of the output gap in the fourth quadrant also deteriorates more rapidly with λ after the turning point (see figure 2.10).

The bottom line is that the case for delegation of monetary policy to a conservative CB is further strengthened. Moreover, the form of the loss function becomes even more symmetrical than before (see figure 2.11), reflecting the increased cost of increasing the weight on output gap stabilization.[10] However, it is also clear that the gist of the results remains unchanged. Indeed, the set of efficient combinations of inflation volatility and output gap volatility corresponds to low weights on output gap (including zero) relative to society's true weight. This is the result we have interpreted before as meaning that only a conservative central banker can be efficient. However, despite the fact that endogenous learning accelerates conservatism, it is still true, as in Rogoff (1985), that the optimal delegation weight from society's viewpoint is lower than society's but greater than zero.

From figures 2.9 and 2.10 it is clear that changes in the constant-gains learning parameter ϕ lead to monotonic shifts in the curves. As the constant-gain parameter decreases, corresponding to increasingly long memories, the results converge to those under RLS. Learning with finite memories amplifies the results under RLS without changing the qualitative features of the results.

2.5   Different degrees of central bank knowledge and information

We will now discuss the sensitivity of the results when the CB's degree of knowledge and information varies. The exercise serves two purposes. The first is to understand, in our simple setting, how the relation between stabilization and stability changes as the CB's knowledge and information about the economy changes. The second is to provide a robustness check relative to the informational assumptions we have made thus far. Indeed, the story told is to a large extent arbitrary. We have talked about the CB being endowed with a HP filter. That begs the question: how dependent are the results obtained on that particular assumption? Would the results change significantly if an alternative filter were applied (perhaps a multivariate filter)? These are very good questions that go beyond the scope of this discussion. Instead of looking at this issue directly we simply consider the continuum of results between the case of perfect identification of the shocks driving the economy and the case considered above (where the CB infers the shocks relying on the HP filter).

We vary the degree of knowledge and information at the disposal of the CB using a very simple device. Specifically, we introduce a new parameter, α. If α equals zero then we are in the case where the CB makes inferences on the basis of the HP filter. If α equals one then we are in the case where the CB perfectly identifies the shocks driving the economy in real time. For the intermediate cases $0 < \alpha < 1$ we assume that the CB has an estimate of potential output which is a linear combination of the two values with weight α. As we increase α the accuracy of the CB's assessment of the current state of the economy improves. It seems to us that this approach enables us to obtain an answer to the first question and to make a tentative first pass at the second. In this section we will always assume that the private sector acts on the basis of the RLS learning algorithm.

The results are portrayed in figures 2.12 and 2.13. The case $\alpha = 1$, in figures 2.12 and 2.13, corresponds to the case which has been plotted before in figures 2.4 and 2.5, respectively. The case of perfect knowledge and information is the most favorable case considered in figures 2.12 and 2.13. For a given weight on output gap stabilization, volatility of both inflation and output are lower than under all alternatives. Taylor's efficiency frontier is closest to the origin, corresponding to the most favorable opportunity set open to the policy maker. The result is intuitive. As stressed at the end of section 2.2 the assumptions made concerning knowledge and information at the disposal of the policy maker are very favorable. The policy maker knows the true structure of the economy and observes the relevant shocks. From figure 2.13 it may be seen that the optimal delegation weight on output gap stabilization is, again as seen before, the same as CGG obtain for the case of RE.

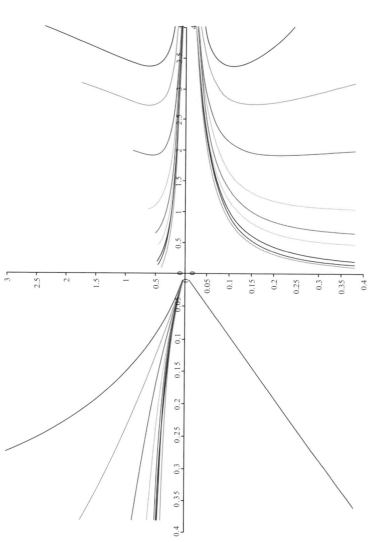

Figure 2.12 From perfect to imperfect information

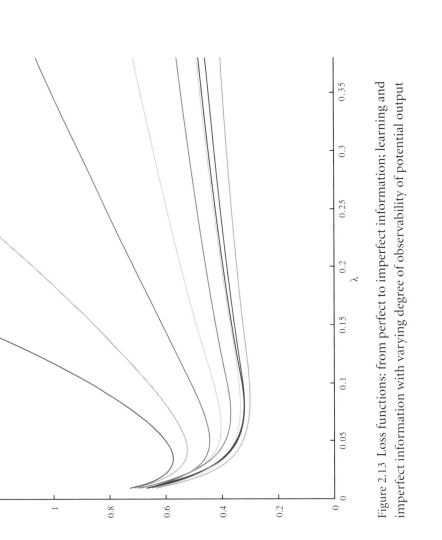

Figure 2.13 Loss functions: from perfect to imperfect information; learning and imperfect information with varying degree of observability of potential output

The case $\alpha = 0$, in turn, corresponds to the RLS case in figures 2.10 and 2.11 (section 2.4). The contrast between the case $\alpha = 1$ and the case $\alpha = 0$ is striking. The discussion that follows relates to section 2.4 but there the comparison was made using an intermediate step allowing for fixed parameters in the algorithm generating private sector expectations. Focusing on this comparison we can make a number of important remarks. First of all, the efficiency frontier shifts sharply up and to the right and changes shape. Indeed, for the case of perfect knowledge and information ($\alpha = 1$) Taylor's efficiency frontier displays a negatively sloped trade-off between inflation volatility and output gap volatility. In the opposite extreme when the CB can make use of the HP only to infer potential output ($\alpha = 0$), Taylor's efficiency bends back. Second, the relation between the volatility of inflation and the CB's weight on output gap stabilization (λ) changes (see top left panel in figure 2.12). Not only does it shift up but also the relation becomes convex. This means that when the CB can make inferences only using the HP filter, it would face faster and faster increases in inflation volatility, with increases in the weight on output gap stabilization on its loss function. Third, the relation between the volatility of the output gap and the CB's weight on output gap stabilization (λ) also changes (see bottom right quadrant of figure 2.12). Clearly the relation shifts down and to the right, showing that output gap volatility increases with λ. This reflects the increased challenge to stabilization policy coming from uncertainty about the output gap. However, the more interesting feature to notice is that the relation is no longer monotonic. Examining the relation more closely one sees that if policy is conducted by a CB with a λ higher than 0.1 – which, in our example, corresponds to the weight on stabilization in society's true loss – volatility of the output gap begins to increase. In this range volatility of inflation and the output gap both increase with λ at the same time. The bending back of the relation between λ and output gap volatility corresponds to the bending back of Taylor's efficiency frontier in the first quadrant of figure 2.12. The points in the positively sloped portion of the frontier are not efficient. It is possible to reduce volatility of inflation and of the output gap simultaneously. Now the set of efficient points – those for which it is impossible to reduce the volatility of inflation and the volatility of the output gap at the same time – corresponds to a value of λ in a narrow range close to zero. Visual inspection suggests a range from zero to about 0.1. Higher values of λ lead to dominated combinations of volatility. In other words, figure 2.12, directly illustrates Friedman's idea that in the presence of imperfect knowledge and information a strong emphasis on stabilization may prove destabilizing. The highest efficient value of λ is precisely the value that leads to minimum feasible output gap volatility. Fourth, turning to figure 2.13, it is again clear that imperfect knowledge and information are associated with a higher loss for all λs. The loss function shifts upwards. It is also clear that the case for conservatism becomes stronger. In fact, not only does the optimal delegation weight on output gap stabilization become smaller, but also the shape of the loss function turns from almost an L (for $\alpha = 1$) to almost a U (for $\alpha = 0$). The asymmetry of the loss disappears when we move to the HP case. All these remarks mirror points already made in section 2.4.

Figures 2.12 and 2.13 make clear that when α varies between zero and one the relation between stabilization and stability varies in a smooth and gradual way. Therefore we see that, by and large, the qualitative features of the discussion are preserved when we consider intermediate cases of imperfect knowledge and information. This is reassuring. It suggests that our metaphor is likely to apply in more general settings. In particular we may conjecture that the assumption of a particular filtering technique (the HP filter) has not played a decisive role. We have therefore tentatively responded to the second question asked at the beginning of this section.

Concerning the first question – how the relation between stabilization and stability changes as the CB's knowledge and information about the economy changes – it is, of course, clearly relevant here too that the relation between λ, on the one hand, and inflation volatility, output gap volatility and society's loss varies in a smooth and gradual way as a function of the accuracy of CB's knowledge and information. Moreover, the optimal delegation weight on output gap stabilization becomes lower and lower as the quality of information and knowledge deteriorates (figure 2.13). However, there are a number of additional remarks for us to make. Figure 2.12 suggests that important features of the relation between λ, on the one hand, and inflation and output gap volatility, on the other, depend on the *size* of the departure from the perfect knowledge and information case. Indeed, it is apparent from figure 2.12, that in our example, only for low αs does the relation between λ and inflation volatility turn convex and its relation to output gap volatility bend back. It is also clear that it is possible to lower α significantly from one without changing the qualitative features of the case of perfect knowledge and information. We interpret this feature as suggesting that if we believe that there are important gaps in the knowledge and information at the disposal of policy makers we will have to consider cases which are not in the immediate neighborhood of the perfect knowledge and information case.

2.6   Conclusions

The theme of this lecture was to explore the way in which imperfect knowledge affects policy makers' ability to pursue active stabilization policies. We have also explored the interaction between imperfect knowledge on the part of policy makers with endogenous expectations on the part of the private sector and examined a set of questions in the tradition of Friedman (and also Rogoff).

To do so we resorted to the simplest model we could, the core of which constitutes a single equation: a New Keynesian or a New Classical synthesis Phillips curve. We considered only one source of imperfect knowledge: that the central banker does not observe potential output directly. It is endowed (exogenously) with a filtering technique and acts on this basis. We have not considered any uncertainty about the transmission mechanism of monetary policy and will abstract from any policy lags. These simplifying assumptions are highly unrealistic but enabled us to keep the story simple and manageable. Moreover, if anything they are likely to tilt the environment in favor of active stabilization policies. Our policy-making institution is not an optimizer but simply follows a number of policy precepts on the basis of perceived economic events. It offsets demand shocks (with complete success), accommodates potential output shocks and manages a trade-off between inflation and output gap volatility for cost-push shocks and level shifts in the private sector's inflation expectations. It does not know the structure of the economy but its judgment about the nature of the linear trade-off, given its perception on potential output, is unfailing. We have argued that the simplifying assumptions are unlikely to bias the results against active stabilization policies. In any case we intend the simple examples we have dealt with above as simple tales to be read as metaphors.

We have seen that when a central bank has to estimate potential output a large weight on output gap stabilization in its loss function may prove destabilizing. All our results were derived through means of simple numerical examples. They illustrate possible outcomes without any claim to generality. Specifically, in our example we have seen that the slope of the trade-off between inflation and output gap volatility turns positive for large weights on output stabilization in the policy maker's loss function. For weights above this threshold there is no meaningful trade-off and the pursuit of price stability becomes a necessary complement to output gap stability. In other words, the set of efficient combinations of inflation volatility and output gap volatility corresponds to relatively low weights on output gap (including zero) in the policy maker's loss function. However, as in Rogoff (1985), the optimal delegation weight on output gap stabilization from society's viewpoint is lower than society's but greater than zero. In our example, the consideration of endogenous private sector expectations through a learning algorithm strengthens the results. In fact the range of efficient weights is further reduced and approaches zero. Moreover, the shorter the private sector's learning window (the more unstable are private sector expectations), the stronger the case for conservatism. However, endogenous expectations do not change the results qualitatively.

Finally, we have examined how the results change as a function of the degree of CB's knowledge and information. We have seen that the results change smoothly and gradually as a function of the accuracy of knowledge and information. In particular, the optimal delegation degree of conservatism increases as the quality of knowledge and information declines. Moreover, we saw that the results were close to the perfect knowledge and information case even when the accuracy of knowledge and information was significantly lowered. We interpreted this result as suggesting that if we believe that departures from perfect knowledge and information are key for the conduct of policy we should be prepared to consider large departures from perfect knowledge. In our view such an approach is further justified if we recall that the examples in this lecture disregarded both policy lags and uncertainty about the transmission mechanism of monetary policy.

Notes

INTRODUCTION

1. Knight (1921), p. 67, footnote.
2. E.g. Allais (1953) and Ellsberg (1961) and the burgeoning literature on behavioral economics.
3. The European Central Bank (ECB) has launched two major initiatives in this direction: the Monetary Transmission Network, whose main findings are summarized in Angeloni, Kashyap and Mojon (2003), and the Inflation Persistence Network.
4. Certainty equivalence always arises when the decision maker preferences are quadratic and the economy can be described by a set of linear equations. On the certainty equivalence principle see, for example, Simon (1956) and Theil (1954, 1957). The most recent, general formulation of certainty equivalence is due to Svensson and Woodford (2004), who show that, for a linear rational expectations model with a quadratic loss function and asymmetric information, both certainty-equivalence and the separation between estimation and control hold.
5. Larson (1999), p. 111.
6. Brainard (1967) is the classical reference on the conservatism principle. Craine (1979) confirms that uncertainty about policy transmission leads to gradualism, but shows that uncertainty about the dynamics of the economy leads to a more aggressive policy. Söderström (2002) also obtains the latter result when uncertainty about the dynamics of the economy concerns the

degree of inflation persistence. Wieland (1998) and Rudebusch (2001) tend to confirm the tendency towards conservatism.

7. Levin, Wieland and Williams (1999, 2003) follow this approach. The two papers analyze backward-looking and forward-looking rules, respectively.

8. The robust control approach has been strongly advocated by Hansen and Sargent (e.g., 2001, 2004) and used by, among others, Tetlow and von zur Muehlen (2001), Giannoni (2002), Kasa (2002), Onatski and Stock (2002), Onatski and Williams (2003). Many of these papers try to identify features of the specification of model uncertainty which lead to more aggressive robust policies than in frameworks that do not take model uncertainty into account.

9. Evans and Honkapohja (2001) have advocated the use of adaptive learning. Most of the literature related to monetary policy has focused on the question of whether the rational expectations equilibrium can be learned using adaptive learning – see, for example, Bullard and Mitra (2002). The results mentioned in the text on the design of policy to avoid instability generated by endogenous expectations have been derived by Orphanides and Williams (2002a, 2003a), Gaspar and Smets (2002), Gaspar, Smets and Vestin (2003) – see also the second lecture in this volume. Cho, Williams and Sargent (2002) show the damage potential of a central bank blindly adopting adaptive learning.

10. The aforementioned references are by no means exhaustive, even to capture the broad directions of the literature. For example, Mankiw and Reis (2002) explore yet another dimension of bounded rationality.

LECTURE 1: MONETARY POLICY IN UNCHARTED TERRITORY

1. See Gaspar, Pérez Quirós and Sicilia (2001) for details.

2. See e.g. von Hagen (1994); see also Deutsche Bundesbank (1999a) for a history of the Bundesbank.

3. See also Issing, Gaspar, Angeloni and Tristani (2001), especially chapter 9.

4. See also Issing, Gaspar, Angeloni and Tristani (2001), especially chapter 4, ECB (2000), and the background studies for the evaluation of the ECB's

monetary policy strategy published as ECB Working Papers nos. 269 to 273.

5. See also Christiano, Motto and Rostagno (2003) and Detken and Smets (2003).

6. See Winkler (2002).

7. See also Smets (2003).

8. See e.g. Goodfriend (1987), Cukierman (1990), Schwartz (1995), Padoa-Schioppa (2002) and the other contributions to the policy panel on "Central Banks and Financial Stability" at the Second ECB Central Banking Conference (ECB, 2002).

9. Taking monetary growth and its interpretation as the starting point both of its monetary policy analysis and of its communications to the public constitutes a significant difference to the procedure of central banks pursuing a strategy of inflation targeting. Those who call the Bundesbank an inflation targeter overlook this important point.

10. See also Gaspar (2000) for an account of the ECB monetary policy actions in the first year of EMU.

11. These include Fagan and Henry (1998) – see also Browne, Fagan and Henry (1997), Coenen and Vega (2001), Brand and Cassola (2004), Cassola and Morana (2003); also Bruggeman, Donati and Warne (2003) and Calza, Gerdesmeier and Levy (2001).

12. See Issing (1997).

LECTURE 2: IMPERFECT KNOWLEDGE, LEARNING, AND CONSERVATISM

1. Milton Friedman (1946, 1947, 1948, 1953a, 1953b, 1961, 1968, 1976)

2. Including Orphanides (2001, 2002, 2003a), Orphanides and Williams (2002a, 2002b, 2003a, 2003b), Gaspar and Smets (2002), Gaspar, Smets and Vestin (2003), Bullard and Mitra (2002) and Cukierman and Lippi (2001).

3. See Angeloni, Kashyap and Mojon (2003) for a review of recent literature on monetary policy transmission with special emphasis on the euro area.

4. Paraphrasing Ludwig von Mises: predicting economic future is beyond the power of any mortal man. See von Mises (1947).

5. Part of this section follows Gaspar and Smets (2002) closely. For a more detailed argument and extensions see Clarida, Galí and Gertler (1999).

6. These remarks illustrate, in the context of a very simple example, the difficulties associated with the definition of unobservable variables such as the output gap. This is particularly the case when the unobservable variables are directly relevant for the conduct of policy. There are in practice two possible reasons that may make it difficult to track down potential output: first the economy may be changing fast. In such circumstances it is difficult to obtain accurate real-term estimates. Second, there is no consensus on how to define and measure potential output. Potential output will depend on the overall model used to define it. In the absence of a consensual model to look at business-cycle fluctuations (see McCallum, 1999) it is unlikely that there will be a common view on the path of potential output even for historical data. Consensus will prove elusive even with the benefit of hindsight.

7. We are using another simplifying assumption. Specifically that the CB controls output and therefore the output gap directly and instantaneously. In a more elastic set-up the CB would control aggregate demand by means of the interest rate. The simplification does not affect the main results we want to focus on.

8. The result is clearly related to earlier findings by Cukierman (2001). Cukierman is interested in discussing the effects of transparency. He considers a model characterized by a Lucas supply function. The CB has some information about the shocks driving the economy. In this setting Cukierman finds that welfare in a fully transparent regime – in which the CB discloses its information on the shocks – is lower than under a partially transparent regime – when it does not. The intuition for the result is that under full transparency the CB cannot improve stability in the economy by means of inflation surprises.

9. The authors are indebted to contributions during the preparation of this section. Gerhard Rünstler for his invaluable comments.

10. Examining figure 2.1 (and comparing it with figure 2.2), there are two important points to highlight. First, the figure illustrates the possibility, emphasized by Friedman (1953a), that counter-cyclical policy may actually increase instability in economic activity. Second, the shape of the

efficiency frontier changes. Under RE there is a well-behaved negatively sloped relation between inflation volatility and output volatility. In the constant-gains learning case the relation bends back and becomes positively sloped leading to a bounded range of efficient insights on output gap stabilization. Values of λ outside that range will increase both the volatility of inflation and the volatility of the output gap.

References

Allais, M. (1953), "Le Comportement de l'homme rationnel devant le risque: critique des postulats et axiomes de l'école américaine," *Econometrica* 21, 503–46

Angeloni, I., A. Kashyap and B. Mojon (2003) eds., *Monetary Policy Transmission in the Euro Area*, Cambridge: Cambridge University Press

Atkeson, A. and L. E. Ohanian (2001), "Are Phillips Curves Useful for Forecasting Inflation?" *FRB Minneapolis Quarterly Review*, 2–11, http://www.mpls.frb.org/research/qr/qr2511.html

Barro, R. and D. Gordon (1983a), "A Positive Theory of Monetary Policy in a Natural Rate Model," *Journal of Political Economy* 91(4), 589–610

——— (1983b), "Rules, Discretion and Reputation in a Model of Monetary Policy," *Journal of Monetary Economics* 12(1), 101–21

Bean, C. (2003), "Asset Prices, Financial Imbalances and Monetary Policy: Are Inflation Targets Enough?" speech at the BIS Conference on Monetary Stability, Financial Stability and the Business Cycle, Basel, 28–29 March

Bernanke, B. S. and M. Gertler (1999), "Monetary Policy and Asset Price Volatility," in *New Challenges for Monetary Policy*, Proceedings of a symposium sponsored by the Federal Reserve Bank of Kansas City, Jackson Hole, Wyoming

Bernanke, B. S. and F. S. Mishkin (1997), "Inflation Targeting: A New Framework for Monetary Policy?" *Journal of Economic Perspectives* 11, 97–116

Blinder, A. (1998), *Central Banking in Theory and Practice*, Lionel Robbins Lecture, Cambridge, MA, and London: MIT Press

Borio, C., B. English and A. Filardo (2003), "A Tale of Two Perspectives: Old or New Challenges for Monetary Policy?" BIS Working Paper No. 127

Borio, C. and W. R. White (2003), "Whither Monetary and Financial Stability? The Implications of Evolving Policy Regimes," in *Monetary Policy Uncertainty: Adapting to a Changing Economy*, proceedings of a symposium sponsored by the Federal Reserve Bank of Kansas City, Jackson Hole, Wyoming

Brainard, W. (1967), "Uncertainty and the Effectiveness of Policy," *American Economic Review* 57, 411–25

Brand, C. and N. Cassola (2004), "A Money Demand System for Euro Area M3," ECB Working Paper No. 39, *Applied Economics* 36(8), 817–38

Browne, F. X., G. Fagan and J. Henry (1997), "Money Demand in EU Countries: A survey," Staff Paper No. 7, European Monetary Institute, Frankfurt am Main

Bruggeman, A., P. Donati and A. Warne (2003), "Is the Demand for Euro Area M3 stable?" ECB Working Paper No. 255, September

Bullard, J. and K. Mitra (2002), "Learning About Monetary Policy Rules," *Journal of Monetary Economics* 49, 1105–29

Calza, A., D. Gerdesmeier and J. Levy (2001), "Euro Area Money Demand: Measuring the Opportunity Cost Appropriately," IMF Working Paper No. 01/179, November

Camba-Mendez, G. and D. Rodríguez-Palenzuela (2001), "Assessment Criteria for Output Gap Estimates," ECB Working Paper No. 54

      (2003), "Assessment Criteria for Output Gap Estimates," *Economic Modelling* 20, 528–61

Canova, F. (2002), "G-7 Inflation forecasts," ECB Working Paper No. 151, June

Cassola, N. and C. Morana (2003), "Monetary Policy and the Stock Market in the Euro Area," *Journal of Policy Modelling* 13, 783–806

Castelnuovo, E., S. Nicoletti-Altimari and D. Rodríguez-Palenzuela (2003), "Definition of Price Stability, Range and Point Inflation Targets: The Anchoring of Long-term Inflation Expectations," ECB Working Paper No. 273, September

Cho, I.-K., N. Williams and T. J. Sargent (2002), "Escaping Nash Inflation," *Review of Economic Studies* 69, 1–40

Christiano, L., R. Motto and M. Rostagno (2003), "The Great Depression and the Friedman–Schwartz Hypothesis," paper presented at the ECB workshop on *Asset Prices and Monetary Policy*, available at http://webint.ecb.de/events/conf/other/assetmp/assetmp.htm

Clarida, R., J. Gali and M. Gertler, 1999, 'The Science of Monetary Policy: A New Keynsian Perspective', *Journal of Economic Literature*, 37(4), 1661–707

Clarida, R. and M. Gertler (1997), "How the Bundesbank Conducts Monetary Policy," in C. D. Romer and D. H. Romer (eds.), *Reducing Inflation. Motivation and Strategy*, Chicago: University of Chicago Press, pp. 363–406

Coenen, G. (2003), "Inflation Persistence and Robust Monetary Policy Design," ECB Working Paper No. 290, November

Coenen, G., A. T. Levin and V. Wieland (2003), "Data Uncertainty and the Role of Money as an Information Variable for Monetary Policy," ECB Working Paper No. 84, forthcoming in *European Economic Review*

Coenen, G. and J. L. Vega (2001), "The Demand for M3 in the Euro Area," *Journal of Applied Econometrics* 16, 727–48

Craine, R. (1979), "Optimal Monetary Policy with Uncertainty," *Journal of Economic Dynamics and Control* 1, 59–83

Cukierman, A. (1990): "Why Does the Fed Smooth Interest Rates?" in M. Belongia (ed.), *Monetary Policy on the Fed's 75th Anniversary*,

Proceedings of the 14th Annual Economic Policy Conference of the Federal Reserve Bank of St. Louis, Norwell, MA: Kluwer Academic, pp. 111–47

(2001), "Accountability, Credibility, Transparency and Stabilization Policy in the Eurosystem," in C. Wyplosz (ed.), *The Impact of EMU on Europe and Developing Countries*, Oxford: Oxford University Press, pp. 40–75

(2002), "Are Contemporary Central Banks Transparent about Economic Models and Objectives and what Difference Does It Make?" *Federal Reserve Bank of St. Louis Review*, July/August

Cukierman, Alex and Francesco Lippi (2001), "Endogenous Monetary Policy with Unobserved Potential Output," paper presented at the NBER research conference Macroeconomic Policy in a Dynamic Uncertain Economy, November/December

Detken, C. and F. Smets (2003), "Asset Price Booms and Monetary Policy," paper presented at the ECB workshop on Asset Prices and Monetary *Policy*, available at http://webint.ecb.de/events/conf/other/assetmp/assetmp.htm

Deutsche Bundesbank (1990), *Monthly Report*, December

(1991), *Monthly Report*, July

(1999a) ed., *Fifty Years of the Deutsche Mark*, Oxford: Oxford University Press

(1999b), "Taylor Interest rate and Monetary Conditions Index," *Monthly Report*, May

ECB (1999), "The Stability-Oriented Monetary Policy Strategy of the Eurosystem," *Monthly Bulletin*, January

(2000), *Why Price Stability?*, proceedings of the First Central Banking Conference, available at http://www.ecb.int/home/conf/cbc1/cbc1.htm

(2002), *The Transformation of the European Financial System*, proceedings of the Second Central Banking Conference, available at http://www.ecb.int/home/conf/cbc2/cbc2.htm

Ellingsen, T. and U. Söderström (2001), "Monetary Policy and Market Interest Rates," *American Economic Review* 91, 1594–1607

Ellsberg, D. (1961), "Risk, Ambiguity and the Savage Axioms," *Quarterly Journal of Economics* 75, 643–69

Evans, G. and S. Honkapohja (2001), *Learning and Expectations in Macroeconomics*, Princeton: Princeton University Press

Fagan, G. and J. Henry (1998), "Long Run Money Demand in the EU: Evidence for Area-wide Aggregates," *Empirical Economics* 23, 483–506

Friedman, M. (1946), "Lange on Price Flexibility and Employment: A Methodological Criticism,' *American Economic Review*, 36 (September), 613–31, also included in Friedman (1953b)

(1947), "Lerner on the Economics of Control," *Journal of Political Economy* 55, 405–16, also included in Friedman (1953b)

(1948), "A Monetary and Fiscal Framework for Economic Stability," *American Economic Review* 38, 245–64, also included in Friedman (1953b)

(1953a), "The Effects of a Full Employment Policy on Economic Policy: A Formal Analysis," in Friedman (1953b), pp. 117–32

(1953b), *Essays in Positive Economics*, Chicago: University of Chicago Press

(1961), "The Lag in Effect of Monetary Policy," *Journal of Political Economy* 69(5), 447–66, also included in Friedman (1969)

(1968), "The Role of Monetary Policy," *American Economic Review*, 58(1), 1–17, also included in Friedman (1969)

(1969), *The Optimum Quantity of Money and Other Essays*, Chicago: Aldine

(1976), "Inflation and Unemployment," Nobel Memorial Lecture, December, Lindbeck (1992), pp. 267–86

Friedman, M. and A. Schwartz (1963), *A Monetary History of the United States*, Princeton: Princeton University Press

Gaspar, V. (2000), "The Role of Monetary Policy under Low Inflation," presentation made at the IMES/Bank of Japan International Conference on The Role of Monetary Policy under Low Inflation: Deflationary Shocks and their Policy Responses, 3–4 July

Gaspar, V. (2003), "Commentary," in *Monetary Policy Uncertainty: Adapting to a Changing Economy*, proceedings of a symposium sponsored by the Federal Reserve Bank of Kansas City, Jackson Hole, Wyoming

Gaspar, V., G. Pérez Quirós and J. Sicilia (2001), "The ECB Monetary Policy Strategy and the Money Market," *International Journal of Finance and Economics* 6, 325–42

Gaspar, V. and F. Smets (2002), "Monetary Policy, Price Stability and Output Gap Stabilization," *International Finance* 5, 193–211

Gaspar, V., F. Smets and D. Vestin (2003), "Private Sector Learning Expectations and Persistence: The Role of the Central Bank," paper presented at the CEPR/BoF Conference, Helsinki, September 19

Gerlach, S. and L. E. O. Svensson (2003), "Money and Inflation in the Euro Area: A Case for Monetary Indicators?" *Journal of Monetary Economics* 50, 1649–72

Gertler, M. (2003), "Commentary," in *Monetary Policy Uncertainty: Adapting to a Changing Economy*, proceedings of a symposium sponsored by the Federal Reserve Bank of Kansas City, Jackson Hole, Wyoming

Giannoni, M. (2002), "Does Model Uncertainty Justify Caution? Robust Optimal Monetary Policy in a Forward-Looking Model," *Macroeconomic Dynamics* 6, 111–44

Giannoni, M. and M. Woodford (2002a), "Optimal Interest-Rate Rules: I. General Theory," NBER Working Paper no. 9419
    (2002b), "Optimal Interest-Rate Rules: II. Applications," NBER Working Paper no. 9420

Goodfriend, M. (1987), "Interest-Rate Smoothing and Price Level Trend-Stationarity," *Journal of Monetary Economics* 19, 335–48
    (2002), "Interest Rate Policy Should not React Directly to Asset Prices," paper presented at the Federal Reserve Bank of Chicago and World Bank Group Conference: Asset Price Bubbles: Implications for Monetary, Regulatory, and International Policies, April

(2003), "Inflation Targeting in the US?" paper presented at the NBER Conference on Inflation Targeting, January 23–26, Bal Harbour, FL

Goodfriend, M. and R. King (1997), "The New Neoclassical Synthesis and the Role of Monetary Policy," *NBER Macroeconomics Annual*, Vol. 12, pp. 231–83

(2000), "The Case for Price Stability," proceedings of the First ECB Central Banking Conference on Why Price Stability? November

(2001), "The Case for Price Stability," in A. Garcia-Herrero, V. Gaspar, L. Hoogduin, J. Morgan and B. Winkler (eds.), *Why Price Stability?*, Frankfurt: European Central Bank, pp. 53–94

Goodhart, C. (1975), "Problems in Monetary Management: The UK Experience," paper presented at a conference organized by the Reserve Bank of Australia, Sydney; also published in A. S. Courakis, *Inflation, Depression and Economic Policy in the West*, Totowa, NJ: Barnes and Noble, 1981

Gordon, R. (1997), "The Time-Varying NAIRU and its Implications for Monetary Policy," *Journal of Economic Perspectives* 11(1), 11–32

Greenspan, A. (1989), Statement before the Committee on Finance, U.S. Senate, January 26

Hansen, L. and T. Sargent (2001), "Robust Control and Model Uncertainty," mimeo, January, available at http://homepages.nyu.edu/~ts43/

(2004), "Misspecification in Recursive Macroeconomic Theory," unpublished manuscript

Issing, O. (1992), "Theoretical and Empirical Foundations of the Deutsche Bundesbank's Monetary Targeting," *Intereconomics* 27, 289–300

Issing, O. (1997), "Monetary Targeting in Germany: The Stability of Monetary Policy and of the Monetary System," *Journal of Monetary Economics* 39, 67–79

(1999a), "The Monetary Policy of the ECB in a World of Uncertainty," in I. Angeloni, F. Smets and A. Weber (eds.), *Monetary Policy under Uncertainty*, Frankfurt: ECB, pp. 20–9

(1999b), "The Eurosystem: Transparent and Accountable or 'Willem in Euroland'?" *Journal of Common Market Studies* 37, 503–19

(2002), "Monetary Policy in a Changing Economic Environment," in *Rethinking Stabilisation Policy*, proceedings of a symposium sponsored by the Federal Reserve Bank of Kansas City, Jackson Hole, Wyoming

(2003a), "Monetary and Financial Stability: Is There a Trade-off?" speech at the BIS Conference on Monetary Stability, Financial Stability and the Business Cycle, Basle, March 29

(2003b) ed., *Background Studies for the ECB's Evaluation of its Monetary Policy Strategy*, Frankfurt: ECB

Issing, O., V. Gaspar, I. Angeloni and O. Tristani (2001), *Monetary Policy in the Euro Area*, Cambridge: Cambridge University Press

Issing, O. and K.-H. Tödter (1995), "Geldmenge und Preise im vereinigten Deutschland," in D. Duwendag (ed.), *Neuere Entwicklungen in der Geldtheorie und Währungspolitik*, Berlin: Duncker & Humblot

Issing, O., K.-H. Tödter, H. Hermann and H.-E. Reimers (1993), "Zinsgewichtete Geldmengenaggregate und M3 – ein Vergleich," *Kredit und Kapital* 26, 1–21

Johnson, H. G. (1971), "The Keynesian Revolution and the Monetarist Counter-Revolution," *American Economic Review* 61, *Papers and Proceedings*, 1–14

Kant, E. (1793), *Concerning the Common Saying: This May be True in Theory But It Does Not Apply in Practice*, English translation by Carl J. Firedrich, in Allen Wood (ed.), *Basic Writings of Kant*, London: Random House, 2001

Kasa, K. (2002), "Model Uncertainty, Robust Policies, and the Value of Commitment," *Macroeconomic Dynamics* 6, 145–66

King, M. (1997), "Changes in UK Monetary Policy: Rules and Discretion in Practice," *Journal of Monetary Economics* 39, 81–97

(2002), "No Money, No Inflation: The Role of Money in the Economy," lecture presented to the First Economic Policy Forum held at the Banque de France, Paris, March 13

Knight, F. H. (1921), *Risk, Uncertainty, and Profit*, Boston/New York: Houghton Mifflin

Kydland, F. E. and E. C. Prescott (1977), "Rules Rather than Discretion: The Inconsistency of Optimal Plans," *Journal of Political Economy* 85(3), 473–91

Larson, E. (1999), *Isaac's Storm*, New York: Vintage

Levin, A., V. Wieland and J. Williams (1999), "Robustness of Simple Monetary Policy Rules under Model Uncertainty," in John B. Taylor (ed.), *Monetary Policy Rules*, Chicago: NBER and University of Chicago Press

(2003), "The Performance of Forecast-Based Monetary Policy Rules under Model Uncertainty," *American Economic Review* 93, 622–45

Lindbeck, A. (1992), *Nobel Lectures: Economic Sciences*, London: World Scientific

Lucas, R. E. (1976), "Econometric Policy Evaluation: A critique," *Carnegie-Rochester Conference Series on Public Policy* 1, 19–46

(1980), "Rules, Discretion and the Role of the Economic Advisor," in Stanley Fisher (ed.), *Rational Expectations and Economic Policy*, Chicago: University of Chicago Press

Mankiw, N. G. and R. Reis (2002), "Sticky Information versus Sticky Prices: A Proposal to Replace the New Keynesian Phillips Curve," *Quarterly Journal of Economics* 117, 1295–1328

Masuch, K., H. Pill and C. Willeke (2001), "Framework and Tools of Monetary Analysis," in H.-J. Klöckers and C. Willeke (eds.), *Monetary Analysis: Tools and Applications*, Frankfurt: European Central Bank, pp. 117–44

McCallum, B. (1997), "Comment," in B. S. Bernanke and J. J. Rotemberg (eds.), *NBER Macroeconomics Annual*, Cambridge, MA: MIT Press, 335–60

(1999), "Issues in the Design of Monetary Policy Rules," in J. Taylor and M. Woodford (eds.), *Handbook of Macroeconomics*, vol. IC, Amsterdam: North-Holland, ch. 23

Mullainathan, S. (2002), "A Memory-Based Model of Bounded Rationality," *Quarterly Journal of Economics* 117, 735–74

Nelson, E. and K. Nikolov (2001), "UK Inflation in the 1970s and the 1980s: The Role of Output Gap Mismeasurement," Bank of England Working Paper No. 148

Neurath, O. (1932), "Protokollsätze," *Erkenntnis* 3, 204–14

Nicoletti-Altimari, S. (2001), "Does Money Lead Inflation in the Euro Area?" ECB Working Paper No. 63, May

Onatski, A. and J. Stock (2002), "Robust Monetary Policy Under Uncertainty in a Small Model of the US Economy," *Macroeconomic Dynamics* 6, 85–110

Onatski, A. and N. Williams (2003), "Modeling Model Uncertainty," *Journal of the European Economic Assocation* 1, 1087–1122

Orphanides, A. (2001), "Monetary Policy Rules, Macroeconomic Stability and Inflation: A View from the Trenches," ECB Working Paper No. 115

(2002), "Monetary Policy Rules and the Great Inflation," *American Economic Review* 92(2), 115–120

(2003a), "Monetary Policy Evaluation with Noisy Information," *Journal of Monetary Economics* 50(3), 605–31

(2003b), "The Quest for Prosperity without Inflation," *Journal of Monetary Economics* 50(3), 633–63

Orphanides, A. and S. van Norden (2002), "The Unreliability of Output Gap Estimates in Real Time," *Review of Economics and Statistics* 84(4), 569–83

Orphanides, A. and J. Williams (2002a), "Imperfect Knowledge, Inflation Expectations, and Monetary Policy," FEDS Paper No. 2002–27, also in B. S. Bernanke and M. Woodford (eds.), *Inflation Targeting*, Chicago: University of Chicago Press, 2003

(2002b), "Robust Monetary Policy Rules with Unknown Natural Rates," *Brookings Papers on Economic Activity* 2002(2), 63–118

(2003a), "The Decline of Activist Stabilization Policy: Natural Rate Misperceptions, Learning and Expectations,"paper presented at the International Research Forum on Monetary Policy, November 14–15, also Federal Reserve Bank of San Francisco Working Paper No. 2003–24

(2003b), "Inflation Scares and Forecast-Based Monetary Policy," FEDS Paper No. 2003–41

Padoa-Schioppa, T. (2002), "Central Banks and Financial Stability," Second Central Banking Conference on The Transformation of the European Financial System, policy panel introductory paper available at www.ecb.int/home/conf/cbc2/cbc2.htm

Persson, T. and G. Tabellini (1999), "Political Economics and Macroeconomic Policy," in J. Taylor and M. Woodford (eds.), *Handbook of Macroeconomics*, vol. IC, Amsterdam: North-Holland, ch. 22

Quine, W. V. (1969), *Ontological Relativity and Other Essays*, New York: Columbia University Press

Rogoff, K. (1985), "The Optimal Degree of Commitment to an Intermediate Monetary Target," *Quarterly Journal of Economics* 100, 1169–90

Ross, K. and A. Ubide (2001), "Mind the Gap: What Is the Best Measure of Slack in the Euro Area?" IMF Working Paper No. 01/203

Rudebusch, G. (2001), "Is the Fed too Timid? Monetary Policy in an Uncertain World," *Review of Economics and Statistics* 83, 203–17

Rünstler, G. (2002), "The Information Content of Real-Time Output Gap Estimates, an Application to the Euro Area," ECB Working Paper No. 182

Sargent, T. J. (1999), *The Conquest of American Inflation*, Princeton: Princeton University Press

Scharnagl, M. (1998), "The Stability of German Monetary Demand: Not Just a Myth," *Empirical Economics* 23(3), 355–70

Schwartz, A. (1995), "Why Financial Stability Depends on Price Stability," *Economic Affairs* 15, 21–5

Simon, H. (1956), "Dynamic Programming under Uncertainty with a Quadratic Criterion Function," *Econometrica* 24, 74–81

Smets, F. (2003), "What Horizon for Price Stability?" *Journal of Monetary Economics* 50, 1293–1309, also ECB Working Paper No. 24

Smets, F. and R. Wouters (2002a), "Output Gaps: Theory vs. Practice," mimeo, European Central Bank

(2002b), "An Estimated Stochastic General Equilibrium Model of the Euro Area," ECB Working Paper No. 171

Söderström, U. (2002), "Monetary Policy with Uncertain Parameters," *Scandinavian Journal of Economics* 104, 125–45, also ECB Working Paper No. 13

Steinson, Jon (2003), "Optimal Monetary Policy in an Economy with Inflation Persistence," *Journal of Monetary Economics* 50, 1425–56

Stock, J. H. and M. Watson (1999), "Forecasting Inflation," *Journal of Monetary Economics* 44, 293–335

Stone, R. (1984), "The Accounts of Society," in *Nobel Lectures: Economic Sciences 1981–1990*, London: World Scientific, pp. 115–139, also available at http://www.nobel.se/economics/laureates/1984/stone-lecture.pdf

Svensson, L. E. O. (1997), "Inflation Forecast Targeting: Implementing and Monitoring Inflation Targets," *European Economic Review* 41, 1111–46

(1999a), "Inflation Targeting as a Monetary Policy Rule," *Journal of Monetary Economics* 43, 607–54

(1999b), "Monetary Policy Issues for the Eurosystem," *Carnegie-Rochester Conferences Series on Public Policy* 51(1), 79–136

Svensson, L. E. O. and M. Woodford (2003), "Implementing Optimal Policy through Inflation-Forecast Targeting," in B. S. Bernanke and M. Woodford (eds.), *Inflation Targeting*, Chicago: University of Chicago Press

(2004), "Indicator Variables for Optimal Policy under Asymmetric Information," *Journal of Economic Dynamics and Control* 28, 661–90

Taylor, J. (1999a), "Staggered Price and Wage Setting in Macroeconomics," in J. Taylor and M. Woodford (eds.), *Handbook of Macroeconomics*, vol. IB, Amsterdam: North-Holland, ch. 15

(1999b), ed. *Monetary Policy Rules*, Chicago: NBER and University of Chicago Press.

Tetlow, R. J. and P. von zur Muehlen (2001), "Robust Monetary Policy with Misspecified Models: Does Model Uncertainty Always Call for Attenuated Policy?" FEDS Paper No. 2000–28

Theil, H. (1954), "Econometric Models and Welfare Maximization," *Weltwirtschaftliches Archiv* 72, 60–83

(1957), "A Note on Certainty Equivalence in Dynamic Planning," *Econometrica* 25, 346–9

Trecroci, C. and J. L. Vega (2002), "The Information Content of M3 for Future Inflation," *Weltwirtschaftliches Archiv* 138, 22–53, also ECB Working Paper No. 33

Vickers, J. (1999), "Economic Models and Monetary Policy," speech delivered to the Governors of the National Institute of Economic and Social Research, London, March 18

von Hagen, J. (1994), "Monetary Union and Monetary Policy: A Review of the German Monetary Union," in P. L. Siklos (ed.), *Varieties of Monetary Reforms*, Boston: Kluwer Academic

von Mises, Ludwig (1947), *Human Action: A Treatise on Economics*, New Haven, Yale University Press

Walsh, C. E. (2003a), "Speed Limit Policies: The Output Gap and Optimal Monetary Policy," *American Economic Review* 93, 265–78

(2003b), "Implications of a Changing Economic Structure for the Strategy of Monetary Policy," in *Monetary Policy Uncertainty: Adapting to a Changing Economy*, Proceedings of a Symposium sponsored by the Federal Reserve Bank of Kansas City, Jackson Hole, Wyoming

Wicksell, K. (1935), *Lectures on Political Economy*, London: Routledge and Kegan Paul

Wieland, V. (1998), "Monetary Policy and Uncertainty about the Natural Unemployment Rate," FEDS Working Paper No. 1998–22

Winkler, B. (2002), "Which Kind of Transparency? On the Need for Clarity in Monetary Policy-Making," *IFO Studien* 48, 401–27, also ECB Working Paper No. 26

Woodford, M. (2003), *Interest and Prices: Foundations of a Theory of Monetary Policy*, Princeton: Princeton University Press

Index